SON OF A WHORE

SON OF A WHORE

FORGING MY PATH TO FREEDOM

Demetrye Isoldi & Elena Isoldi Medici

AWAKEN
VILLAGE
PRESS

This is a work of nonfiction. Any resemblance to persons living or dead should be plainly apparent to them and those who know them, especially if the author has been kind enough to have provided their real names. All events described herein are all true from the author's perspective.

The content of this book is for general instruction only. Each person's physical, emotional, and spiritual condition is unique. The instruction in this book is not intended to replace or interrupt the reader's relationship with a counselor, physician, or other mental health professional.

Copyright © 2020 by Demetrye Isoldi & Elena Isoldi Medici
All rights reserved.

Printed in the United States of America.

Editing by Awaken Village Press
Cover and interior design by Tim Murray and Daniel Holloway

ISBN 978-1-7344265-8-8 (paperback)

Library of Congress Cataloging-in-Publication Data

Published by Awaken Village Press, Sioux Falls, SD

www.awakenvillagepress.com

CONTENTS

Introduction — ix
It's About Love — 1

SURVIVOR

In the Beginning — 5
Lula Mae — 9
Tessie Mae — 13
In the Pursuit of Happiness — 17
Childhood Lost — 27

CHASING LOVE

The Grass Is Greener — 33
Cowboys and Indians — 43
Unhappily Ever After — 51
The Good, the Bad, and the Ugly — 57
Without a Trace — 73
Turning Point — 79
Forbidden Fruit — 85

TRUE LOVE

Green Eyes — 99
Learning to Love — 107
Love Returned — 113
Made to Last — 117
Black Man's Hair — 129
Meet the Russians — 133
Put a Ring on It — 137

MISSING PIECES

Far From the Tree	143
More Than a Whore	155
A Name of My Own	165
A Legacy of My Own Making	171

FREEDOM HAS A COST

Point of No Return	181
One Day at a Time	193
At Her Cost	199
Here Comes Our Miracle	207
Saving Grace	217

A MAN OF MY OWN MAKING

Happily Ever After	223
Shedding Skins	233
There Is Nothing to Forgive	243
But There Is Room for Forgiveness	257
The Gift of Love	271

I dedicate this book to my two angels sent to this Earth to help me become the man I am today. My two loves—my wife and my daughter. Without you two, neither my life nor this book would be possible.

I also dedicate this book to every hurt, abused, abandoned, and neglected boy and girl, man and woman. To each person who ever felt like a bright, peaceful, and love-filled life was not meant for them. Nothing can be further from the truth. There is a fountain of life, peace, and love hidden deep within your soul. I hope you unlock it with what you find on the pages of this book to become the creator of your happiness and success.

To love somebody is to let them become
the highest version of themselves.

Elena Isoldi Medici

INTRODUCTION

"Why did you want to write this book, Demetrye?" she asked me at ten o'clock one night, emerging from the bathroom, hair still dripping wet after a shower.

"What?" I mumbled as her voice yanked me out of sleep.

My wife is not like most people. While I am barely functioning at this hour, this is when her creative muse comes to inspire her ... almost every night. After all this time, I still have not gotten used to the late-night pillow talks as she calls them.

"Why did you write your book, Demetrye?" she repeated.

Peeling my eyes open, I jerked my brain into reality knowing that fighting this would be a losing battle. When my wife wants something, she goes after it like a hungry dog after a bone. She will chase after it six ways from Sunday until she gets it. And once she does, she becomes a happy, relaxed, smiling, drooling-over-her-bone pup. I figured I might as well concede and play along.

Pulling myself up into a sitting position, her face only inches away from mine, I stared at her.

The manuscript has just been completed. We were in pre-publishing phase and now she wants to ask this question?

Okay, I will play along, I thought to myself. *Maybe I can still manage to get some sleep tonight if I do.*

"Because I want to touch people's lives," I responded. What could be better than that? How grand of me! I am a purpose-driven man! That would get her off my back and my head back to the warm pillow I just abandoned.

"I call BS!" she said.

My eyebrows raised now. I should be used to this. We have been together for almost half of my life—nearly twenty years. I feel my mind being challenged and stretched, so I take the bait.

"I want to give people hope. People who, like me, were abandoned, abused, hurt ... "

"Let me stop you there," she interrupted without apology. "I call BS on that too. That might be one of your motivations, but you are going too broad. Too far. Did you really write this book for 'the people?'"

"Yes ... ?" I responded, now doubting myself. I felt like I was being set up for a test that I was guaranteed to fail.

"Give me your journal and a pen," she commanded.

I handed the said items to her. I knew that we were in for a wild ride. Fighting it would be useless. My personal K-9 was after a bone, and I would be a fool to get in the way of her hunger.

"Okay, let's talk through it until we get to the truth." she said.

Something inside me had a feeling that she already

INTRODUCTION

knew the truth, but in Elena-like fashion, she was not going to do the work for me. I am still surprised how this woman manages to know me better than I know myself.

Deep sigh. I conceded.

"Let's do it."

"WHY MY BOOK?" she wrote at the top of the page. "Talk to me."

"I am an overcomer, Elena," I responded. "I wanted to talk about overcoming trauma, abuse, betrayal, betraying. I want to give people, like me, hope that if I could create a better life for myself, so can they."

"That's good. But that's not it," she pressed. "You are still going too broad. Go inward instead. Go smaller scale."

I was getting impatient, so I threw her a few more responses, hoping it would get her off my back, but they did not land.

Exasperated, she finally threw me a bone, "Why did you write this book for *yourself*?"

I had never thought about it that way. The entire time I was writing, I felt I had been driven by a big purpose. So big that I would become a world changer; to help at least one person who has gone—or is going through—a mess similar to mine see a brighter future. But did I really write it for that person? Now she had me questioning myself.

"Would you just tell me?" I finally asked.

"No way!" she protested. "You have to uncover it on your own."

And then it happened! Clear as day, the truth emerged.

While I had the intention and hope to help others, I wrote this book first and foremost for myself!

It was cathartic. Writing each word in this book was cleansing and liberating. I opened my life like a book to be read—first to myself, then by others, so there were no more secrets or doubts. I became vulnerable for the first time in my life, hiding no sin and asking for no pardon. It was my confessional. It was cleansing to admit to my faults and to my victories.

But it went deeper than that.

"Keep going, darling," she was gentler now. "Give me more."

Four more pages of the journal filled up with her larger than life scribbles.

"I wanted validation. I wanted meaning." I was becoming the dog chasing the bone now. I could not stop. I felt that I was getting so close.

"Meaning in what way? Get validation from whom?" She was coaching me to my own discovery as she has done thousands of times with her clients.

"I wanted to prove to my mother that I am worthy of living. Worthy of loving," I said, my heart swelling with emotions. I had a mother-size hole in my heart my entire life that I still wanted to fill. A hole that would drive me to chase after the affection of women while simultaneously distrusting any woman who dared to be close to me. A hole that would have me protect my abuser even in my adulthood, while subconsciously still seeking her approval. I still desired her love.

"And? What else?" Elena prodded further.

Up until Elena began to encourage me to start writing my story, I was never one to think that my life was something so special that it needed to be shared or have a book written about it. I was raised in a broken environment as are millions of others. My parents abandoned me, but millions of others share the same plight. I made horrible decisions that nearly cost me everything as millions of others did and still do. Every. Single. Day. So, nothing made me special. At least not my pain or my failures. Millions of us are hurting.

INTRODUCTION

Daily. Humanity shares pain and suffering as a common denominator. Millions of us are failing. Daily.

Yet something in me yearned to tell my story, my truth. But I was scared. In fact, at first, I hid parts of my story because I felt ashamed—ashamed of what happened to me and ashamed of what I did.

It took me years to find the courage to begin writing. Years to push myself to put pen to paper. Years to become honest with myself to the degree you will find in this book. I still desired approval from the woman who raised me, my ultimate mother figure, so much that making the decision to write this book caused me deep agony. What if she judged me when she read it? What if my book infuriated her? What if … ? Just playing out possible scenarios of her responses in my head caused me anxiety and left me feeling paralyzed. Somewhere, deep inside of me, still lived a little boy who desired his mother's approval, and, subconsciously, he was making my decisions for me. So I procrastinated. Torn between fear and desire to write, I waited.

Then one day, I knew it was time. I had to write it. Not because of the pain. Not because of my failures. And not even because I wanted to punish those who hurt me. Rather, the opposite.

I needed to write it because maybe it could serve someone just like me. Perhaps my story could give someone hope that they too can overcome fear, rejection, abuse, and self-loathing to create whatever life *they* were brave to imagine.

I had to write it because I was fortunate to have found a way to rise above the pain, abandonment and neglect; above the agony I experienced and the agony I caused. Because even though I had all the reasons to give up and become a byproduct of my upbringing, I made something of my broken life. I wrote it because I finally found the courage to break through the fear of rejection by the woman who raised me and take my power back.

And then, sitting less than a foot away from my wife in the middle of the night, the truth came out of me like the rushing of springtime river waters breaking through ice.

"I wrote it because I wanted to leave a footprint on this world. I wrote it because I *matter*."

"There," she said, fully satisfied. "You got it."

I sat in the quiet of our bedroom. Now, not the least bit bothered that she woke me. I felt this revelation drop deep into my gut and explode like the Fourth of July fireworks.

"I wrote it because I want to matter," I whispered to myself. There was no going back to sleep. I had to sit in this newfound awareness. Understand it. She sat back, smiling with smug satisfaction.

If there was one thing I learned in my life, it was to trust Elena. You will see why on the pages to come. For now, suffice it to say, if she felt this deeply about me finding my truth, my ears were open to hear.

I wrote this book because my story is like the story of millions of boys and girls, men and women who were stripped of their ability to dream and feel safe, to trust and love, and to share their truth without the fear of judgement and rejection. I wrote it for you because, like me, you might have carried your pain with you through your formative years into adulthood and were defined by it. I wrote it because, despite your pain and struggles and hopelessness, you need to find hope that your life can have a miraculous turning point. A point that would give you, and all of us, a chance to stop the cycle of pain instead of passing it down to generations to come as it has been done unto us. A point that would give you meaning.

INTRODUCTION

I wrote it because even though we are broken, neglected, rejected, hurt, and abused, we can still find the power in us to unleash meaning, purpose, peace, and wholeness into our lives. Not despite the pain we lived through, but because of it.

And when we do, we can finally accept each part of ourselves without shame or judgement so we can release our hearts, minds, and future from the grip of our abusers and our past in order to become whole, as if we were born again.

And, in some ways, I wanted to write this book for my biological mother and the woman who raised me—a mother-like figure who is still alive. Not to expose or shame those who had done me wrong, but to show them, and myself, that I matter! I wrote this book to share a story of hope and transformation. A story of redemption. A story of defining and forging my own path to freedom and unconditional love.

I wrote this book to show that we are not responsible for the choices of our parents, our abusers, and those who have wronged us. We are not responsible to cover for them or to conceal their misdeeds while suffering in painful silence because we were taught by religion, society, and our parents that we *must* forgive. The freeing reality, which I will share with you in this book, is that the choice of what we do with our past is left up to each of us. We can either continue to live in pain and shame, or step outside of our conditioning into acceptance of our past as a vehicle toward our ultimate joy and healing.

I wrote this book to remind you, dear reader, that it is us who get to write the final chapter—not those who brought us into this world or who raised us; not their expectations, failures or opinions. Even the most hopeless of us can turn our lives around, heal our brokenness, heal our dysfunction, and create the most beautiful lives for ourselves that we never dreamt possible.

I wrote this book because I lived both as a victim and a villain before I found my way to freedom. I found a way to purge myself from pain, guilt, hurt, abuse, shame, and judgement. I found a way to love, loyalty, success, and hope. And if I can do it, so can you.

Finally, I wrote this book to tell *you* that *you matter*! Your story is worth being told. There is nothing that you endured, no matter how dark or painful, that cannot be used to propel you forward and make *you* the creator of your own destiny.

To protect identities of people still living, some of the names in this book have been changed.

LOVE
IS A
TRICKY
EMOTION.

IT'S ABOUT LOVE

ALL SHE wanted was to be loved. A bastard child of a married man who already had eleven mouths to feed, she was an unwelcomed addition.

Her mother had nine children by seven men. An invalid after a stroke at the age of thirteen, she could not keep her. So she was given away to a family who might give her a better life.

She was abandoned, and she felt it. Never fully fitting in. Never a sense of belonging. She wanted to be loved. She longed for acceptance and adoration. Since a young age, she looked for love by seeking it out where she might find it. Shuffling through men like a deck of cards. Many of them. Often. But none filled the void.

In her mid-twenties, two kids in tow, she ran away from a failed relationship, stealing away her children in a pursuit of love and a better life … for herself.

A woman in appearance, a child inside, crying out for love, with no understanding of what love was. She would pass down the same agony to her children. They too will long for her love, acceptance, and adoration. They too will be left wanting.

Like a litter of unwanted kittens, they were often left behind with strangers while she was on the prowl, searching for the next hit of her drug of choice. Desperate to feel something. Anything. With men. Many of them. Often.

Each time, as she would head out the door, her youngest, barely three, would scream: "Mommy, don't go! Please! Please don't go!" But she would not stop nor give as much as a glance back at him on her way out.

He too would never know what a mother's love feels like. Left with strangers, always feeling alone. Always afraid. His surroundings constantly changing.

But her pursuit was not about him or his sister, who wasn't even five at the time. This was her time to find love, acceptance, and self-worth, not the time to be in the business of giving love, taking care of the lives she created, or behaving like a mother should. How could she possibly give her children what they craved? She never knew what love of a parent felt like. She could not give them what she did not possess.

Love is a tricky emotion. People die for it, live for it, start wars over it, and sacrifice so much for it. She was willing to give up everything she possessed to quench her thirst for it.

Her name is Tessie. She is my mother. And this is our story.

PART ONE

SURVIVOR

THE FIGHT FOR
MY LIFE DID NOT
START AT BIRTH—
IT STARTED AT
CONCEPTION.

ONE
IN THE BEGINNING

THE APPLE doesn't fall far from the tree, they say. If my mother's birth was framed with rejection, mine was with both rejection and violence. Although, the fight for my life did not start at birth—it started at conception.

My father was one of many men my mother used in an attempt to find love. Boy meets girl. Girl wants to be loved. Boy and girl hook up and before you know it, girl is pregnant with her second child. Girl is scared. Girl tries to abort the fruit of her lust. On her own. With a wire hanger. That was my glorious coming into this world. Against all odds, I made it!

Lucky? Lucky I was not. But one thing I was—a survivor.

When it comes to memory, our brains process trauma more intensely than happiness. The more intense and emotionally charged the pain we experience, the deeper the pain will lodge itself into the lower parts of our brain that process emotion. Traumatic experiences get stored across deeper layers of the brain and are not likely to be erased by future experiences. So, it is no wonder that I am able to recall memories from my early childhood.

One of such memories I have is of my father when I was not even two. I was crying inconsolably. His frustrated face hovering above me, filled with anger, powerless to comfort a crying child. Then a pillow coming over my face, pressing me into the mattress, and my world going dark.

I am a survivor.

I was born with a gaping father-and-mother-sized hole in my heart. Much like my mother, I looked for love in many places. Never feeling whole. Never quite fitting in.

I was born in the projects of Savannah, Georgia, where the division between Blacks and Whites, poor and wealthy, free and slaves, ran rampant for two hundred years prior to my birth.

Settled in 1733, Savannah, the first city in the state of Georgia—the final American colony—was supposed to be the first place where there would be no "lawyers, slavery, or rum." However well-intentioned it was and despite a ban on African slavery, by the late 1740s slaves were openly sold in Savannah, and the slave trade was officially legalized by 1750.

It was sometime around then that a ship filled with slaves from West Africa landed on the shores of Georgia, bringing my ancestor to America.

A free woman became a slave. Forced into a life of servitude. Stripped of her human rights. She bore a child by her English master. And that child bore another one, who bore another, and down the line until a young woman named Sarah was born. She was my great-great-grandmother. After surviving generations of slavery and abuse, Sarah became a free woman and started a family into which, one day, I would be born.

By the time I made my way into this world, I was not only a survivor of my mother and father's violence, I was a survivor of a two-hundred-year history of violence that was still raging in Savannah against my people.

I would spend the next forty years fighting for my place in this world and for my right to be free from pain, abandonment, prejudice, and to quench my thirst for love and acceptance. Whether it was the fierce Blackfeet and Cherokee warrior blood in me, the cry of African slaves that longed for freedom no matter the cost, or my humanity, I allowed nothing to hold me back from achieving this goal. Even if it would cost me everything.

BUT, AS ALL
LIVING BEINGS,
SHE YEARNED
FOR LOVE.

TWO

LULA MAE

My mother, Tessie Mae McPherson, was born on September 28, 1955, to Lula Mae Grant and James Thomas.

I don't know much about my grandfather, except that he had thirteen children and stepped out on his wife frequently. One of his illicit affairs resulted in producing Tessie—a transgression he would rather ignore than embrace. However, little as I was when my mother fled her violent union with my father, and I was torn away from my biological family, my brain stowed away some memories of my grandmother.

Once, Tessie, my sister Kat, and I took the Amtrak train from New Jersey to Yemassee, South Carolina, to see Grandma. I remember her charging toward me, with a mug in her hand to give me a hug. THUNK! Her mug unintentionally collided with my head as she drew me in. Maybe because it hurt or maybe because it was one of so few memories I had of my family, but I could never forget that moment, even though the time erased her features from my young mind as the years passed on.

Lula Mae had a hard life. At the age of thirteen, she suffered a stroke, paralyzing the right side of her body. It also stole her ability to communicate clearly, affecting her speech. In addition to her physical affliction, Lula Mae could not be called a natural beauty, which made things even harder for this young, defenseless Black girl. But, as all living beings, she yearned for love.

Her afflictions and her thirst to be desired made her vulnerable. Like vultures, men swooped in, one after another, promising her what she wanted most, only to take advantage of her. Most left their seedlings in the wake of their affairs.

Nine children by seven men.

Given her physical limitations, Lula Mae could not take care of her children alone. An invalid, she depended on others to help rear her little ones, but help was not easily found.

During the times of slavery, families were often torn apart to fatten a master's wallet, not allowing deep bonds to form between mother and child. It might be because of this that it became culturally acceptable in the parts of Yemassee, where Lula Mae lived, to give one's children away to be raised by others. Whether due to this or her physical and financial hardship, Lula Mae and her mother decided to place her children with other families.

One after another, Lula Mae sent her babies off to be raised by neighbors, distant relatives, and any good people that would take them. My mother, fourth in line, was placed with Sadie and Jimmy Aikens, a kind-hearted couple who could not have kids of their own. They had already taken in another child to raise, named Liza. Tessie and she became adopted sisters. The two would grow to share a very peculiar bond.

As seeds thrown to the wind, each of Lula Mae's children grew up separated from her. Yet, amazingly, as if being drawn by some invisible force, all of them came back to their mother once grown, one by one. They gathered, as chicks to their mother hen, to take care of her and reconnect with each other. Could it have been the purity of Lula Mae's motherly heart or the children intuitively knowing that she never wanted to part with them? It's a mystery I will never uncover, but the family eventually reunited and formed a deep bond that only blood relatives share.

My mother, however, could never seamlessly fit back in, as if she was a missing puzzle piece from a different set. She always yearned for more than her adopted and biological families could offer. More than her hometown could give her. Glamour. Love. Life. Opportunities.

She wanted more and let nothing stand in her way.

WITH A GAPING HOLE IN HER HEART ONLY LULA MAE AND THOMAS WERE MEANT TO FILL, SHE WOULD NEVER GET OVER BEING GIVEN AWAY.

THREE

TESSIE MAE

TESSIE MAE had a way of standing out in the crowd. She had a passion for fashion. A woman with a taste for the finer things of life and social flair, she craved and loved attention. Outgoing, engaging, beautiful, and a dreamer. Yemassee was too small of a town to contain her, as was Savannah, where she was raised and met my father.

By the age of fourteen, Tessie already knew her way around men. With a gaping hole in her heart only Lula Mae and Thomas were meant to fill, she would never get over being given away. Even though she was raised by two people who loved her, Tessie felt rejected and was angry, hurt, and thirsty for acceptance that Sadie and Jimmy could not give her, although they tried.

At fifteen, Tessie played fast and loose with a man eleven years her senior by the name of John. By sixteen, she became a mother, something she neither had the skills nor desire to be. So, much like Lula Mae, she felt it better to commit her child into someone else's care and left her with Sadie Aikens—the woman who raised her. (But this is something I wouldn't learn about until I was eight.)

Tessie was not ready to settle in the poverty-stricken part of Savannah where she was raised. She wanted to see the world, so she enlisted in the Navy. With high hopes and ready to find a better life, at the age of seventeen, Tessie was off, leaving her parents, her family, and her baby daughter behind.

She served her time and was in the Reserves by the age of twenty-one when she moved back to Savannah. There she met a strapping young man named Edward Charles Wilkins, with as much sense and maturity as hers.

Edward, born in Savannah, Georgia, in 1954, was a man-child. He had two infatuations—women and martial arts. Earning an honest living was not his calling. Having fun and pleasure was his religion. He would go to extremes to avoid a responsible adult life.

Unlike Tessie, Edward came from a more stable background. Oldest of six, he was raised by both parents. He had a doting mother—ever the peacemaker who saw nothing but the best in her children, even when they did not justify her blind motherly love. His father, on the other hand, had a violent temper. He was known to beat his boys until he sank into stupor, got tired, took a nap, then came back to "discipline" them more. Faithfulness was not in Grandfather's vocabulary—he stepped out on Grandma more times than she would admit. Yet she stayed.

Tessie was not Edward's first love nor his last. He was attracted to her boisterous and colorful personality. She was infatuated with the possibility of being in love. But because he was incapable of giving her the glamorous life she desired, Tessie did not feel like he was the man who deserved her, so they never tied the knot.

Their life was turbulent and often violent. They got into screaming matches and physical fights. But while they clashed on many things, it was their desire to live a fun-filled life that united them.

Nights of passion and parties between Tessie and Edward ended up in an unplanned pregnancy. Not wanting another child, she opted to have an abortion. Months later, pregnant yet again, for reasons unknown, she decided to keep the baby. This is how my sister Kat came into the world.

Neither contraception nor the sanctity of creating life was something to which my mother gave much thought. To her, life and the responsibilities that came with it were disposable. Two more abortions—each time a set of twins. At twenty-two, I was conceived. Another mistake, she decided not to keep. But by the time she made up her mind, no doctor would perform an abortion. In desperation, Tessie grabbed a wire hanger, stuck it into herself, and tried to dig me out, piece by piece.

By some grand design, I made it!

It would take another year and a half of her love-hate relationship with my father, a year and a half of abuse and neglect by both of them, and more abortions (twelve in total during her relationship with Edward), before Tessie would decide that the relationship and her time in Savannah were over. She thirsted for more from life, but neither her children nor Edward nor her hometown could quench that thirst.

SHE WAS A
WHORE AND
DID NOT HIDE IT.

FOUR

IN THE PURSUIT OF HAPPINESS

TESSIE NEVER settled down. She never found a place to belong. Not with her biological or adopted families, not with her multiple lovers or my father, and seemingly not even with the children she reluctantly brought into this world. Underneath fancy dresses and a pretty face hid a woman with a hollowed-out space in the shape of a heart. A space she craved to fill with love, adoration, and attention, but unfortunately not from the tiny people she created in the pursuit of happiness.

She wanted a grand life. But while success-driven women of her generation went to college and worked hard to make it in the male-dominated world, Tessie took a different approach. She was determined to find her golden goose—a man to provide for her physical and financial needs. Finding one worthy of having her was her primary goal. In her mind, it was like playing the lottery. However, my father, Edward, did not have the winning numbers. As time passed, he became more like his father—mean and violent. Not even two years old, I nearly died when he smothered me with a pillow because I would not stop crying. But I was not the only one to receive his wrath.

Fed up with his violent outbursts and lack of financial support, Tessie had an itch to leave Georgia. The final straw that pushed her out the door was walking in on Edward molesting my sister. Momma Bear awakened in Tessie that day. She grabbed a knife and stabbed him in the back. Packing her bags in a hurry, she grabbed Kat and me, boarded a Greyhound bus, and stole us away to find a better life.

Destination: Elizabeth, New Jersey.

As the wheels of the Greyhound bus sped her closer to her new home, Tessie hoped that, along with Edward, she was leaving behind her failed attempts at finding love and happiness and that her luck would change. However, unbeknownst to her, with every turn of the wheels, Tessie was headed into more tumultuous waters. She did not know that love will always evade her. That happiness would always remain elusive because she would never realize that she was looking for it in places where it could never be found.

While a thriving and diverse town, Elizabeth had poverty-stricken areas. The ghettos were predominantly filled with Blacks and Hispanics, peppered with some Italians and Irish. Broke and unemployed, this is where Tessie landed. The parts of town where police sirens blared several times a day, folks on the street screamed and argued nonstop, prostitutes made their living while their pimps handled them and their clients, and drug dealers hooked the poor, young, and uneducated on illicit drugs. While she didn't want to admit it, this is where Tessie belonged.

Still refusing to settle, she dragged Kat and me throughout Union County, hopping from one bus to the next, one house to the next, one bed to the next, one man to the next. Stability was a luxury Kat and I were not afforded. Barely two and three years of age, we were at the whims of our mother's decisions, frequently moving from one place to another daily.

In the pursuit of love and happiness, Tessie Mae felt that she had something to prove to the world and particularly to men. While Lula Mae was a conquest to be had by men, her daughter proudly carried a banner of retribution for all that her mother had endured. Tessie was the conquistadora with a string of men shuffling in and out of her life. Short relationships, one-night stands, one-hour stands—she had them all. She would give herself to each one fully while, at the same time, keep her power, deciding who could stay and who had to leave immediately after her sexual thirst had been quenched. While craving to feel the love she never received as a child, she was determined to be the one in control of giving and taking it away. In doing so, she decided how involved they would be in her life and by extension ours. It was not unusual for her to commit even us, the ones who depended on her for their safety, into the hands of these men. This came at a high cost to Kat and me.

One man's name is forever etched into my mind—Quincy. Tessie would frequently liaison with him. He had her directive and full permission to discipline me as he saw fit. The form of discipline they had in mind was not time-outs or losing privileges to things that already did not exist in my life. He was tasked with beating me with a belt until my toddler-sized brown body would turn blue.

A total stranger taking violent ownership of me, whipping me for things that any other toddler would get away with, left me feeling trapped and helpless. Each time Quincy unleashed his wrath on me, while wincing in pain, all I could think was: "Where are you, Mom? Shouldn't you be here to stop this? Please, I beg you, make this stop." However, Tessie did not come to my rescue. She did not hear my cries. For a long time, I hoped that I would wake up from the horrible dream called childhood, from feeling betrayed and find myself in an embrace of a loving mother, not an indifferent whore.

Tessie did not need to outsource her violence to others. She was up to the task herself. She beat us frequently with anything she could get her hands on in a hurry—switches, extension cords, wire hangers, Wiffle Ball bats, wooden sticks. The beatings were accompanied by a barrage of insults and profanity, so the trauma and pain went more than skin-deep.

One day at one of our many temporary homes, I stuck a wire hanger into an outlet out of curiosity. Sparks and fire came out. While entertaining to behold, I was scared. The man of the house pulled me away just in time to avoid getting electrocuted. As a four-year-old, I felt barely escaping with my life was punishment enough, but Tessie didn't see it that way.

When she got home that night, she dragged me out of bed and stripped my clothes off. Getting beat naked was a requirement with Tessie. (And yes, it is beat, not beaten.) While still very young, I was well aware that there was no way to avoid Tessie's wrath. Naked and at her mercy, I silently begged for the punishment to be over fast. Locked and loaded, Tessie was ready. She grabbed me violently, bending me over her knees with a cord rhythmically landing on my back, legs, and behind.

"DIDN'T-I-TELL-YOU-NOT-TO-GET-IN-TROUBLE?!" She shouted as the cord smacked my flesh. "DIDN'T-I-TELL-

IN THE PURSUIT OF HAPPINESS

YOU-TO-STOP-BEING-A-STUPID-LITTLE-SH*THEAD?!"

The furious blows came in a steady stream, making my skin burn as if a vat of boiling oil was spilled over my body. The beating ended when Tessie finally got tired and needed a break. I jerked away from her to safety, my body feeling like chunks of skin were torn off of me, tears pouring down my cheeks, too afraid to cry out in pain. Doing so would have provoked Tessie even more.

I was not the only victim of Tessie's abuse. A simple act of disobedience would easily result in Kat getting stripped naked, her tiny body pushed into a dirty mattress as our mother would straddle her, pressing her down and beating her anywhere her hand, a belt, or a hairspray bottle could land. Scared and knowing I might be next, I would hide myself in the darkest corner, praying she would not see me while blinded by her rage. I would not be so lucky. When she was done with Kat, she would yell:

"Dee, come here!" And then my world would go dark.

That same woman would then go to church, sit us next to her on the pew, and testify to others how good God had been to her and her children. There was nothing sacred to Tessie. The same hands that beat us within an inch of our lives several times a week would be raised to the heavens in praise every Sunday. Kat and I were inconvenient mistakes, ones she resentfully kept and ones she could not terminate in time as she had done with our never-to-be-known siblings.

Tessie was not in the running for Mother of the Year. She was a whore and did not hide it. While prostitutes, just outside our door, sold their bodies for money, Tessie gave hers away for free. Maybe for pleasure, or perhaps in an attempt to fill the void in her darkened heart, since her pursuit of happiness was not yielding desired outcomes. While looking for love, she was filling her bed with what she could get at the moment. Short, tall, drug addicted, alcoholics, and once, even an unwashed handicapped homeless man. She would bring them into our space, strip them down, and copulate with them in front of us, often without so much as a warning to tell us to look away or cover our eyes and ears. Sounds, images, and smells of her salacious affairs were burnt into our minds and cannot be forgotten. Kat and I witnessed things that no children should ever see.

To escape the lewdness of our reality, Kat and I would cling to each other, cradling each other's bodies as tightly as we could, disconnecting our minds from reality, imagining we were in safer homes, surrounded by people who loved us. On occasion, Kat and I would watch cartoons—our connection to a more peaceful world. But even these moments were stolen from us. It would not be long before we would hear Tessie tell us to keep looking forward and not turn around, while yet another grotesque fool, dripping with sweat and stench of the ghettos, would mount and ride her on the very same bed.

Four years of hell with no end in sight. Eventually, Tessie found a dilapidated apartment over a storefront church that we would call home for a while—the longest residence we had while living with her. A three-bedroom, two-bathroom structure we shared with another family of five. The three of us stuffed into one room with a soiled mattress on the floor as a makeshift bed. The only piece of furniture in the room was a chair to hold our prized possession—a black and white TV with rabbit ear antennas. Our neighbors were poor but decent people. Parents Harry and Louise, and their three kids Angie, Tamara, and Tony, close to our age.

Living on a busy street infested with prostitution, drug dealers, and gangs, it was never safe to go outside. We were prisoners in our own home. Thin walls allowed every noise from the street to invade our daily existence. Broken windows, chipped tiles, broken faucets, and stained toilets—a place that was only safe for cockroaches and rats. And there were plenty of those. Rats, the size of bowling balls, strutted through our apartment as if they owned the place along with a cockroach population that could not be curbed even with copious amounts of Raid. We always had to be on high alert.

Life with Tessie was always tense. We never knew what would set her off. One wrong move and we might receive one of her infamous beatings. So, we did our best not to upset her. The only times we felt we could let down our guards were when Tessie would leave the house, sometimes for a few hours, sometimes for a few days, doing what I imagine she did in front of us. Under Louise's observing eyes, we could be kids again while playing with her children. But even then, Tessie's shadow lingered over us. We acted out what we had learned by watching our mother, with our neighbors' kids.

Once, Kat was caught with Tony in the bathroom reenacting Tessie's wildest nights. Both so young, they did not know what they were doing. Both were punished, with Kat beat to a hair of her life once Tessie got home. Albeit a little younger, I was not exempt from curiosity. I too acted out my mother's escapades. Once with Angie, and once, at school in kindergarten, laying behind a sweet little girl. Not that I could do much with the little body of mine at the time, but like a crazed dog in heat, I air humped behind her, emulating my mother and her lovers.

While lacking stability, safety, and comfort, Tessie's sex obsession was the only constant in our lives. She never slowed down, her perversity rising to a strong crescendo that eventually had to break.

One day, I found myself a victim of my mother's insanity. Lying next to me on the stained mattress, with wind howling outside, she drew my body near hers, but not like a mother should. She pressed her mouth into mine and began to kiss me. I had seen her depravity, often forced to witness silhouette shows of her and the charity cases she called men reflecting on the walls of our one room apartment. But this was something I did not expect.

My mother never showed her affection for me this way before. I did not know what to make of it. The kiss felt good. Is this what mother's love feels like? I was curious about the meaning of it. But curiosity quickly turned to repulsion. Deep inside it felt wrong. I wanted none of it. I wanted to escape. I wiggled my way out of her grip, puzzled, and concerned. We turned away from each other and fell asleep without her saying a word.

Even though her preying on me was a one-time occurrence, I would judge myself many times even into adulthood for the mixed feelings and curiosity I experienced then.

Her depravity was only superseded by my shame and at times, hunger. Louise, in the absence of our mother, sweet as she could be, would make us cheese sandwiches on the same counters that were sprayed with Raid. I would be too scared to eat the food and too scared to turn it down—what if Tessie heard of my ungratefulness? "Thank you," I would say, and then hide my hands under the table, throwing my sandwich for the rats to find. Luckily, Kat and I were enrolled in a kindergarten at this time where we could have a meal that was not laced with dirt and poison. I would rush to school, my stomach growling, to devour whatever snacks they would give us.

Kindergarten was my haven, a welcomed reprieve from my daily nightmare. Playing with kids, eating food safe for consumption, and not being beat for simply being alive gave me the emotional break I needed to survive. Having to be alert at all times, I did not feel safe to be a child around Tessie. School is where I could let my guard down, step out of the protective shell that I retreated into while at home, and become the happy energetic self I was born to be—playful and living in the moment. But even there, Tessie's shadow still lingered over me.

Once I fell off the monkey bars and was taken into the nurse's office. One of the two nurses in the room had me take off my shirt to inspect my body. In addition to the scratches from taking a fall, my back was covered with welts and bruises from my most recent beating.

"What happened, Demetrye?" she queried.

"Oh, nothing. I fell," I responded, nervously pulling my shirt back on, in case they talked to Tessie. I knew I might get beat for saying anything that didn't please her. My survival instinct was to cover up for her misdeeds. By this age, I knew her triggers well and stayed clear of them as best I could. Neither of the nurses pressed for more or followed up with Tessie.

Tessie's cruelty scarred me more deeply than the welts on my back. Not speaking up for myself and doing what I could to please others to avoid pain and rejection would linger over me for much of my developing years. Being called on by a teacher, a classmate, or an employer would create anxiety and fear. "What did I do wrong?" would be the first thought crossing my mind. It started with Tessie, then it was reinforced by other authority figures in my life and lasted well into my thirties.

I WAS BEGINNING
TO REALIZE
THAT WE WERE
A BALLAST SHE
COULD NOT WAIT
TO CUT LOOSE.

FIVE

CHILDHOOD LOST

Kat and I were very close while growing up. We were born only a year and a half apart. When Tessie would leave us for days in abandoned houses or with strangers, vanishing into the streets and locking the door behind her with nothing to eat, Kat took care of me. She nurtured me in the best way a five-year-old could and made sure I did not starve. She would search through the cupboards for a morsel of food to sustain our tiny bodies.

Kat was a young girl who looked after her brother the way her mother was supposed to. She was my momma bear. She made sure I was safe. The weight of the world was thrust on her tiny shoulders; still, she didn't buckle. She had no choice but to step up and relinquish her childhood, overtaken by her maternal instincts.

Once we were left alone at Tessie's friend's house in Newark, New Jersey, a very dangerous crime-ridden town where you do not go outside unless you know someone who could protect you. We woke up on a dirty mattress thrown on an old metal bed frame with a growling dog that seemed more like a wild beast staring at us. With nothing but a flimsy gate separating it from us, we were scared to move. Any attempt we made to go to the bathroom or get food was met by the dog barking so viciously that saliva would fly out of the sides of its mouth, scaring us back onto the bed. Hours passed, our tiny stomachs growling before help in the form of Tessie's friend Cynthia, came to our rescue.

At one point, while we were still less than four and six respectively, Edward reentered our lives. I will never know if he came for us or to be with Tessie. While she was not keen on getting back with him, he moved to New Jersey anyway and was granted visitation rights. Any normal, loving mother would have fought to keep a monster like him away after the atrocity he committed against her daughter, but Tessie permitted it to happen.

One day, as he picked us up for his weekly visit, he must have decided it was retribution time—Tessie was about to find out what he felt when she stole us away. He grabbed Kat and me, boarded a Greyhound bus, and took us to Savannah. No clothes, no food, no plan. We were at his mercy. Would he be a better alternative to Tessie? Scared and helpless, we hoped so.

It did not take more than a couple of days, however, before we were in the same situation—left home alone, locked up without food while Edward was out being chased by his demons. Two days went by before someone realized that there were kids locked in the house without adult supervision. The only reason we did not starve was because Kat found a few slices of bread to feed us until we were discovered. When the police showed up at the door, she was scared but present enough to remember the phone number of Tessie's adopted sister who lived in New Jersey. Following her intel, the police reached out to them. After days of searching, this family tracked down Tessie. She came down to Georgia to save us from his hell only to deliver us back to the one of her making.

Whether with Tessie or Edward, we had no one to turn to. No one to check on us. Orphans with two living parents. Being survivors was in our blood. Whether it was because Tessie was a very private woman or because our aunts and uncles were busy with their own lives, none of them ever bothered to check on our wellbeing. Even if they suspected something, nothing was done to change our circumstance. Growing up I often wondered if they simply did not care about us.

Turning to each other as two abandoned kittens would for love and comfort, Kat and I became inseparable. Because of this Tessie endearingly called us "Mutt and Jeff," based off of characters in a long-running and widely popular American newspaper comic strip. Kat was my everything. She was my calm in the midst of an all-encompassing storm of our lives. She was always there for me no matter what happened. As long as she was near me I was happy.

Kat and I were both stripped of our childhood and coped with it in our own ways. Kat learned to survive with her reality by quickly losing herself in play with other children when Tessie was gone. I, on the other hand, went inward. Never relaxed enough to feel at ease. Always aloof. Always looking out the window, checking for safety—a habit I formed that would last me well into my adulthood. When Tessie left on her escapades, I would spend hours sitting in a corner, waiting for the door to open and my mother to walk back in and save me, love me, need me, despite her proven track record.

Little as I was, I often wondered if Tessie really wanted us. Never showing affection, brutally beating us while rhythmically peppering her beating with profanity, always leaving us behind. I was beginning to realize that we were a ballast she could not wait to cut loose and that the only chance I would have at stability, love, and security would have to be found elsewhere.

PART TWO

CHASING LOVE

I WANTED THEIR
ADDRESS, THEIR
HOME, AND THEIR
LOVE TO BE MINE.

SIX

THE GRASS IS GREENER

KAT AND I were thrown around in the wind of Tessie's life, never knowing where we would land next yet always praying for a respite for our little souls. By some grand design, in the midst of our daily storms, there was an occasional harbor as if an answer to our tear-stained prayers. It was the house of Liza and John Brown, my mother's adopted sister and her husband, where we began to visit on occasional weekends. We called them Aunt Liza and Uncle John.

Liza and Tessie were raised by the same family. Both adopted. Sisters through nurture not nature, their lives could not have turned out more differently. While both had bigger better plans for their lives than their humble beginnings, Tessie escaped her parents' home in search of love as a reckless teenager, while Aunt Liza was more level-headed. She met a man she liked, found a way to his heart, got married, and moved up North where Black men had better opportunities to make a living to support their families.

Uncle John was born in Claxton, Georgia in December of 1920. Raised in the Jim Crow South when people of color didn't own much, he never allowed sinister laws of poverty and segregation to hold him back. By the 1940s, he had two houses—one he built for himself and the other for his mother. Married early, he and his first wife had two children. Loyal to a fault, he would have spent the rest of his life with her, but she had taken to the bottle and left him to raise their babies on his own.

Shortly after, a Black Southern belle thirteen years his junior entered his life. She knew how to reach his suffering heart. She knew how to take care of him and his two children. Before long, after courting and with their parent's blessing, Aunt Liza became his wife. A man of few words, he allowed her to bring his weary soul back to life, and with her ever encouraging belief that he can do anything, Uncle John decided to move his family to New Jersey in the pursuit of a better life for his children and his new bride.

While illiterate, he found a way to build a well-respected tire business that exists to this day, now run by his son. A hard worker, never to shy away from any labor, he would get up at the crack of dawn, get his hearty breakfast and a cup of coffee, grab his lunch, and head out for a long day at work, returning at seven o'clock at night.

Uncle John's exterior, all six-feet-one-inch of him, with rough hands smelling of grease and oil from fixing car tires all day long, was tough and masculine. When I first met him, he seemed like a giant to me, a man you would not want to cross in a dark alley. But once I got to know him, he was a kind man who I never heard use so much as a harsh word with his wife.

An offspring of a slave from the West Indies, he knew how to work hard to provide for his family. While he did not know how to read or write—a skill he outsourced to his able wife—he certainly knew how to make and save money. He never trusted banks, keeping his savings in a locked closet at home. Only one key. Not even his wife had access to it. And he never trusted doctors. Neither did he believe in taking time off work. Once a heavy tire fell on his leg and broke his knee. Instead of taking time away from his business to tend to it, he toughed it out, going on with his day. As time passed, the knee healed, but Uncle John was left with a limp for the rest of his life.

Aunt Liza, a social butterfly raised in Savannah, knew what Southern hospitality was all about. She loved to be around people—meeting new ones, while keeping old friends taken care of and happy. Plump and pleasant, she was a fulltime housewife who knew how to throw down a great soul food meal. Though easy going and forgiving, she was a force to reckon with if things did not go her way.

Uncle John and Aunt Liza had five children: Bobby, Anne, and Roger along with Geri and Tom—kids from John's first marriage. Those two were already grown and living on their own by the time we came on the scene.

When Aunt Liza and Uncle John first entered our lives, and we inserted ourselves into theirs, I was only eighteen months old. How we met was unforgettable to Uncle John, who was quite a storyteller.

"One Sunday, before church," Uncle John would tell the story of our first meeting, with much disgust in his facial expression, "your mother showed up at our house with you and Kat. You were hungry, tired, and dirty. Your diaper was filled to the brim with shit and you stunk. You two looked like orphans."

SON OF A WHORE

At first, when we moved to New Jersey, Tessie felt that Aunt Liza did not approve of her life choices, so she distanced herself. As time passed on, Aunt Liza and Uncle John, out of pity for us, opened their doors for more frequent visits from Tessie and her brood.

Unlike our unstable daily conditions, often filled with putrid smells, dirt, cockroaches, and rats, the Browns' home seemed like a place that belonged on a postcard. Clean, warm, and furnished. The smell of plastic that covered their couches to keep them in a pristine condition became a holy aroma in my nostrils each time I came through the doors.

Hard working people, they took pride in their possessions. House so clean with freshly vacuumed carpets, it would pass a white-glove inspection. Each time we came for a weekend visit we were greeted by the smell of fried chicken, collard greens, mashed potatoes, mac and cheese, and sweet potato pie. The signature smell of these meals would hook Kat and me by our nostrils and drag us straight to the kitchen. The smell of abundance. No need to throw away my Raid-laced cheese sandwiches to feed the rats. I could eat this food without the fear of poisoning myself.

Sunday mornings would take this euphoric experience to another level. We would wake to the sounds of Gospel music filling the air. "Lord, I Am Available to You," "Where Is Your Faith in God?" and "Ain't No Need to Worry"—these songs are permanently etched into my mind as sounds of joy, peace, love, and warmth.

Aunt Liza, busy in the kitchen making breakfast. Bacon sizzling on a cast iron skillet, pancakes getting flipped at a skillful turn of her wrist on an electric grill.

"Dee, Kat, it's time to get up," would sound her cheerful voice as the most welcoming alarm. We would rush to the kitchen to see the table barely containing the bounty of food Aunt Liza lovingly prepared for the entire family. We would pile our plates with grits, eggs, bacon, drowning our pancakes in Aunt Jemima syrup, and filling our glasses to the brim with orange juice. This was the dream life!

When breakfast was over and dishes cleaned and put away, it was time to get ready for the service. It was church time! I was off to wash my face in a clean sink, get my teeth brushed, hair combed, and put on a suit, tie, and my shiny church shoes.

Excited, with my natural kid curiosity, I would peek into Uncle John's room as he would unlock his closet, pull out his three-piece suit, don it on, slick his hair back with S-Curl No Drip Activator, and spritz himself with Old Spice aftershave. A vision to behold—he was the image of manliness. He was my first example of what a man should be like: strong, handsome, protective. I felt safe with John, quite the opposite of my experience with Edward.

Aunt Liza would not be outdone. Her best Sunday dress on and a church hat firmly attached to the head so it would not slide off during praise and worship, high heel shoes on her feet—we were ready for church.

All seven of us would pile into the family van for a day of service. And a day it was. Aunt Liza was a pastor of a small Black church of about twenty-five people. Uncle John was the head deacon. Their kids made up the band with Bobby on bass, Roger commandeering the drums, and Anne welcoming God into their midst on the piano.

Much like most African American churches, Aunt Liza's congregation took church seriously. The morning was filled with praise and worship with songs often spontaneously erupting from the congregation. Clapping and dancing, arms raised in praise, followed by testimonials and offering time. After about an hour and a half—Scripture reading and announcements.

Pastor Brown preaching fire and brimstones, bringing down the house with the power of the Word peppered with praise breaks and shouting. Deacon Brown sitting in a chair, unphased that his wife was leading the congregation, teaching a sermon, holding an office higher than his.

With time, I learned that to be the norm in the African American churches. Women could be as strong as they wanted to be without apologies or excuses while Black men felt safe and secure in their masculinity. This contrasted a lot of other cultures I observed where the church communities were and still are predominantly led by men, and women are expected to submit while being treated as inferiors in one way or another when it comes to spirituality.

After the fiery sermon, back to more testimonials then closing remarks. Then benediction. Three hours later we were ready for a lunch break.

We would pile into the van and head off to KFC to refuel. Most of the congregation would meet there where adults could chat while the kids played after a hearty meal. Then back to church for the evening service. More praise and worship, more testimonials, another offering, sermon, benediction, and closing remarks. Happy and exhausted we would be back home and in beds by ten at night.

This was the life. One of stability, predictability, and no wondering "what's next?" and I wanted it for myself for the rest of my life. There was a routine in the Brown household that was missing in our lives. It was welcoming, comforting, and peaceful. It gave me a sense of normalcy and safety. There was always a warm meal, a bed with clean sheets, and a pillow on it for me. A clean bathroom without broken tiles, rusted mirrors, rusty rings in the toilets, or broken faucet handles and with warm running water. The bare essentials for many, yet a luxury for me.

The Brown family loved television. TV time was how the family connected. It was the center of their daily lives. Soap opera shows for Aunt Liza during the day as she tended to the household. Uncle John, after a long day of fixing tires, would relax in his brown La-Z-Boy recliner rubbing his large hands clean from dirt and grease watching John Wayne movies. Meanwhile, I would nest my four-year-old body between his legs using them as my driving sticks pretending I was in a race car. His legs were my safety from the world, my guards and protectors from turbulent times with Tessie. They were the antidote to my daily uncertainty. *The Jeffersons* and *Good Times* shows during dinner time, and me falling asleep to beer commercials in the evening. Instead of beatings, the television rhythmically and predictably measured out my time with them.

Much like being at school, when I was around the Brown family, my guards were down. I could be a kid. I could mentally relax from the tension and fears of being around Tessie. I could live in the moment, and I savored every single second of my time with them. It was safe to go outside and play on the street with other kids. Meeting up with Stevie, a boy about my age who lived across the street, to play in the front yard was my favorite pastime.

Kat and I would run to Fourth Ward Park to play under Anne's watchful eye. Swing, slides, and playing ball were our most treasured activities.

Unlike Elizabeth, Linden was safe and peaceful. The street the Browns lived on was something out of The Andy Griffith Show—a Black version of the little town of Mayberry in many ways. Kids playing outside on their own. Everyone knew their neighbors and was involved in each other's lives. Taking pride and ownership in their neighborhood, they kept it safe. No drugs, sirens, or prostitution in sight.

The Browns had everything I wanted. I loved visiting Aunt Liza, Uncle John, and their grown kids. I wanted to be around them. I wanted to live with them. I prayed often to become one of them. I wanted their address, their home, and their love to be mine. I begged God for a miracle to have this family call me their own. It would take years, but eventually my prayers would fill up the cup of my suffering and overflow to result in an answer that was nothing short of a miracle.

I WAS WILLING
TO GET MY LOVE
FROM WHOEVER
WAS WILLING TO
GIVE IT.

SEVEN

COWBOYS AND INDIANS

OVER THE next couple of years, Kat and I would spend more and more time at the Browns' house. While I looked forward to our weekend getaways, Kat still clung to Tessie as if trying to suck out any possible maternal love Tessie might have possessed, perhaps intuitively feeling what the future had in store for us. I, on the other hand, reveled in the possibility of having stability and a cozy house, although I also felt torn—I wanted to be with my sister. However, the desire for safety and predictability had proven to be a more powerful emotion.

As far as I was concerned, if there was a way to exchange Tessie and her maniacal behavior for a soul that would be excited to have me, love me, and give me security, then I was willing to let go of whatever notion of family that existed between me and my mother. The Browns were my dream family. They had everything I ever wanted, so I was going to take any chance I got to live with them and to feel like one of them. And, maybe one day, call Aunt Liza and Uncle John "Mom" and "Dad."

Anne, who was only sixteen when we came into her life, fell in love with us, and especially with me. Years later, I would find a dedication certificate listing her as my godmother. She, not Tessie, would be the one taking Kat and me to the park to play on the swings. During our weekend stays, it would be her putting me to sleep, tucking me in, wishing me good night. She even wrote me a lullaby that I still sing to my daughter:

Go to sleep, baby.
Close your eyes, baby.
Close your great, big beautiful eyes.
And when you wake up, baby,
You will have a beautiful surprise.

Each night, drifting off to sleep, the only surprise I dreamt of was living with Anne and her family. It was Anne who seeded the idea in Aunt Liza's mind to invite Kat and me to live with them permanently.

"But who would take care of them?" Aunt Liza would ask. She was already in her fifties, and Uncle John in his late sixties.

"I will, Mom!" pleaded Anne. "They need us, and I love them."

Whether it was my innocent charm, Anne's begging, or Uncle John and Aunt Liza realizing that Kat and I had no future if we stayed with our mother, one day they asked us if we would like to move in permanently.

They had a conversation with Tessie who was all too eager to agree to the arrangement. She would no longer be weighed down by us. She could go anywhere she wanted, be with anyone she desired, and never think about the two beings that were tying her down. She was all in! She agreed to let us go, as long as she could visit and take us for occasional weekends.

My prayers and my wildest dreams were answered! I could finally break away from the abuse, beatings, and neglect. While Kat was reluctant to leave, it was a resounding "YES!" from me. Without hesitation I moved in with them as fast as I could so they would not change their mind.

Kat, on the other hand, stayed with Tessie. Her transition would be slower than mine. Despite the abuse we endured, my sister was very close to our mother. While we both desired love, we wanted it in different ways. Kat wanted that love to come from her mother. She still wanted Tessie to wake up one day, leave her tumultuous life behind, and become the mother Kat desperately needed and deserved. I, on the other hand, wanted out. I didn't want to suffer any longer. I was willing to get my love from whoever was willing to give it.

It tore my tiny heart to pieces when Kat and I were split between two homes. When she was not there, I felt like a piece of me was missing. Despite all of this, I had to make peace with what was.

I never regretted my decision. Coming home from school daily to the Browns' house gave me such a feeling of peace and bliss. I never wanted to leave. Stability was what I needed to thrive.

Like a tornado, Tessie would demolish these wonderful moments when she picked me up to spend weekends with her. She still stayed in Elizabeth, in the one room shack.

While living with the Browns allowed me time to feel safe, each time Friday rolled around I was awash with anxiety, fearing what the weekend with Mom would have in store. I no longer wanted Tessie. All I wanted was to be with my new family. Knowing that they would be there for me was the only reason I was able to survive those weekends.

Despite such brutal interruptions, my life was moving forward. I was now in first grade, but because of abuse and malnourishment in my early years, my development was delayed. I didn't communicate well for my age. It would take years for me to catch up to the same level of mental astuteness as my classmates.

One Christmas, while still bouncing between the Browns and Tessie, Anne came to pick Kat and me up from our weekend with Mom. Tessie bought me a toy for Christmas—a Cowboys and Indians set. Whether she did it to buy my love because I was quickly slipping out of her control, or perhaps, for a moment, she felt something in her heart that was akin to maternal love, either way she drew a bargain that she thought would be hard to refuse.

"Demetrye, if you stay with me for Christmas, I'll let you play with Cowboys and Indians tonight," she offered. "And if you don't, you'll have to wait until our next weekend together to play with it."

I would not be swayed. I might have been young, but I was clever enough to recognize manipulation. I chose to wait, or never have the toy at all, and spend the holiday with the people who loved me rather than cave in and endure Tessie longer than necessary. Even though she did not want us, that day Tessie experienced the pain of rejection she inflicted on us so frequently, which made her want to have control over us even more. She experienced a lot of rejection in her life—first by her biological parents, then by a string of her lovers. This might have been the reason she kept pushing Kat and me away—punishing us for the sins we never committed just to have a sense of power in her life. *"Do unto others before they can do it unto you"*—a hurt heart's cry that would manifest itself even in my life years later. She could not bear the pain of rejection. So she pleaded, threatened, and bargained. But I remained unmoved.

That Christmas with the Browns was glorious. They did not believe in spending money on real Christmas trees, so each year an artificial tree would be brought up from the basement. It would be unboxed ceremonially, pulled out, and spread to its full standing glory. Then the kids would be given full license to decorate it any way they wanted. That year Anne, Kat, and I got the honors as Uncle John and Aunt Liza sat in their chairs grinning ear to ear, watching us experience a real Christmas for the first time. There was no specific theme, much like the *Christmas Story* tree. Multicolored lights, silver garlands, toys from ages before went up hanging as high as we could reach. A white piece of linen on the floor to imitate snow. To my six-year old mind, this was the most beautiful tree in the world.

Aunt Liza spent the Christmas season making soul food as people piled in and out of the house to share in the holiday cheer. Christmas gifts towered around the tree, spilling into the hallway, making it hard to maneuver. But we did not mind—we never had experienced such abundance in our lives.

Christmas day became my favorite day of the year. That year, like many years after, we woke up to find Aunt Liza and Anne already busy in the kitchen, prepping for the biggest event of the year—Christmas Dinner! Turkey, mashed potatoes, collard greens, candied yams, corn bread, mac and cheese, cranberry sauce, apple, and pumpkin pies with ice cream were to be served up with Georgia-style sweet tea and cherry and grape Kool-Aid with enough sugar to make it taste like syrup.

Bobby, Roger, Kat, and I would spend most of the day playing games and peeking into the kitchen, salivating over the feast to come. Bing Crosby would be belting "It's beginning to look a lot like Christmas" on the radio, while *A Christmas Story* played on TV. This movie became my lifelong obsession, transporting me back to those sweet moments I had with the Browns. That year I melted into what childhood is all about—being fully present, lost in the moment, afraid of nothing, in anticipation of everything.

Unlike most families, we would not open our presents until after dinner time. All day we were filled with anticipation for food and gifts. Like a good American family, when dinner time rolled around we overstuffed our bellies with food so good it would make you wanna slap your momma and tell your daddy to get out.

Then, while halfway in a food induced coma, we opened the presents. The smell and sound of the gift wrap paper was intoxicating. G.I. Joe, a basketball, and a pistol were among the many presents I got that year. I felt like I had died and gone to heaven! Toys! For me! I was allowed to be a child and play with whatever I received immediately, and they were mine to keep. No ultimatums. No bargains or threats. Cowboys and Indians were not even a thought in my mind, although eventually I got them too.

By 10 p.m., exhausted from excitement, yet too wound up to fall asleep, we were ushered to brush our teeth and get ready for bed. This was a Christmas I would never forget and would measure all Christmases to follow against it.

In contrast, the times with Tessie became more turbulent. As I spent more time with the Browns, she became more jealous and irrational. She didn't like that Kat and I were getting gifts, shown love, and given attention. So, when we spent time with her, she would lash out even more violently and beat us without provocation. In fact, it felt like she was looking for a reason to unleash her maniacal wrath on us.

Kat struggled with a developmental delay. She used to peel paint off the walls and drag it into her mouth. One time, while visiting with us at the Browns', it set Tessie off more than usual. She dragged Kat to the basement and beat her across the mouth with a stick. When they returned upstairs, Kat's lips were bloody and torn. While everyone in the house heard what was going on, no one intervened, because in the Black community you don't challenge the mother. Mother's always right, even when she is deadly wrong. Despite this cultural code, Anne worked up the courage to speak up and confronted Tessie.

"Mind your business!" Tessie snapped back. "As long as they are my kids, I will discipline them the way I see fit."

Kat and I knew that while Tessie was around, we were never safe. Like a sword of Damocles, she was hanging over our heads. Ever present. Always threatening our peace. One wrong move and her fury could be unleashed.

On one of our weekend visits, Tessie got me a yellow Wiffle Ball bat and ball. I refused to take the gift, fearing that taking it would prevent me from going back home to the Browns. She placed it into my hands, but I threw it down. Tessie flew into a rage. She picked up the bat and beat me with it. No amount of screaming or begging would stop her. After a few minutes, I shut down. Checking out of reality, I imagined being back in the warmth of Anne's embrace. Rather than giving into momentary childhood excitement, much like with Cowboys and Indians, I chose temporary suffering to ensure permanent love and freedom.

"I LOVE YOU, MOM,"
I WHISPERED TO
HER FOR THE LAST
TIME IN HER LIFE.

EIGHT

UNHAPPILY EVER AFTER

I was spending most of my time with the Browns, while Kat was still with Mom. Tessie still found ways to manipulate Kat into not leaving her. When she saw me on Sundays, Kat would say, "You look so good and taken care of," with a longing in her eyes that were saying more than her words could convey. She was missing me as much as I was missing her.

Kat, now almost eight, was often left to spend nights alone in Tessie's dilapidated apartment. Kat could never get a wink of sleep, afraid of the sounds outside and rats and roaches on the inside. Her nights were filled with terror. Any sound in the house or on the street would fill her with anxiety. After debaucherous nights, in the wee hours of the morning, Tessie would show up, finding Kat exhausted and trembling in fear.

A few months after I moved out, Kat finally found the courage to tell Tessie she wanted to leave too. The Browns opened their home to receive her. A clean bed was prepared for her in the same room as me. Finally, Mutt and Jeff were reunited and closer than ever.

We saw Tessie on and off for the next couple of years. She visited the church we attended and occasionally dropped by unannounced at the Browns'. During one such visit, Tessie announced that she was getting married. She finally found the man of her dreams—Michael Owens. At last her dreams came true and her efforts paid off! He was a working man. Someone who could take care of her. She was certain she had won the lottery. She now was ready to settle down and build a life with him. Tessie wanted Kat and I to be in the wedding.

On the day of the wedding, all dolled up, we entered the church. To our surprise, we were treated to a reunion with our Southern family—Tessie's siblings, nieces, and nephews were in attendance. At last, she could prove to them that dreams do come true. Kat and I were too shy to approach them. So it was not until the day after the wedding, when Tessie and Michael came to the Sunday service that for the first time in our lives, we learned that we had a sibling. A teenage girl, who looked much like Tessie, stood to greet us with a timid smile on her face.

"Kat, Dee, meet your sister Etoy," said Tessie.

Was it a joke? We knew nothing about this girl. We had a much older sister! Shocked and lost for words, we did not know how to act. So, we spent the rest of the day avoiding Etoy and saw her only once more before she faded from our lives.

Tessie reemerged only a few more times in the next year. Once, to let us know that she was pregnant. I even got to feel our baby sister kick when Tessie took my hand and placed it on her belly. To feel her move filled me with excitement.

UNHAPPILY EVER AFTER

I felt happy to have another sibling and hoped she would not face the same fate as Kat and me. Unlike with us, Tessie awaited this child with a lot of anticipation. She did not seem like the same woman who raised us. However, her joy was short-lived. She had a stillborn. The irony of this situation does not escape me—there was me, a survivor of a failed abortion, and there was my little sister, who was wanted, but did not make it. Heartbroken, Tessie felt like her life came to an end.

Her life with Michael was also crumbling. With time, things got bad enough for her to leave him. She moved in with the Browns for a short time. They gave her access to the basement, where she spent her days in silence, rarely coming upstairs. On the last day I would ever see her, she was sleeping on the living room couch. My room was not too far, so I was awakened when she groaned in her sleep. I walked to the couch and watched her for a while. It seemed like she was in pain. At breakfast as she passed by, I quietly pulled her in giving her a kiss on the cheek. "I love you, Mom," I whispered to her for the last time in her life. The following day she left for Yemassee, never to be seen again.

In May of 1990, just as I was about to turn eleven, something unusual happened. Anne came home and took Kat to the corner store near our house to get a treat. When they got home, it was my turn to go for a ride. As we pulled over to the same store in the family van, Anne offered to hold my hand. She proceeded to tell me that Tessie had passed away without sharing any further details. She watched for my reaction, ready to comfort me. However, instead of grief I felt a sense of relief. The reign of Tessie's terror over Kat's and my lives was over. She could no longer hurt us. I didn't shed a tear. No sign of grief. The nightmare of abuse and neglect was over.

At the age of thirty-four, Tessie was to be buried in the place she spent her entire life running away from—Yemassee, South Carolina. She would be surrounded by the people she shunned—her siblings and Lula Mae.

The entire Brown family—Uncle John, Aunt Liza, Bobby, Anne and Roger, and Kat and I—packed into the family van and made the long journey from New Jersey to South Carolina to bid farewell and pay respects to the woman who deserved no respect at all.

Tessie Mae was as unforgettable in death as she was in life. When we walked into the church on the day of her funeral, we saw a pink and bronze casket. Tessie was going out in style. The casket was closed, and I was grateful for it. I did not want to see her dead. And frankly, I was scared. There was a part of me that wanted to remember her alive although I shed no tears over her dying.

Kat and Etoy sat next to each other on a pew, crying. I sat next to them, unmoved. Her death still did not seem real. Anne leaned over and whispered that it was okay to cry. However, the only thing I could focus on was wishing for the casket to remain closed.

Much to my dismay my prayers were not answered. The casket was opened, and there laid my mother. She was wearing a white dress and white gloves; her large bi-focal glasses, which she wore as long as I could remember, on her face. My heart dropped as I stared at her body from where I sat. I couldn't move. The gravity of reality began to sink in. The woman who wanted me dead from the moment I was conceived and created a living hell for me, was making her way to a purgatory of her own.

After the sermon, farewell messages, and some hymns, Anne took me to the casket to say goodbye to Tessie. Still scared to see her body up close, I could only raise my hand slightly to wave my last goodbye.

After the burial, Aunt Liza insisted on whisking us away. Lula Mae wanted to spend time with the grandkids she barely knew, but her request was denied. Liza, as she would do so many times in the years to come, said "No." Using traveling back as an excuse for an early departure, we left. It seemed like there was bad blood between the Browns and the Grants that we were too young to understand. It would take me almost fifteen years to find out what it was. I saw Lula Mae's face filled with pain, as she waved goodbye to her late daughter's kids, never to see them again. That night, instead of getting back on the road, we went out to eat and spent the night in a hotel.

Well into my adulthood, Tessie's death was shrouded in mystery. No one would tell Kat and me what happened for her to die so young. At the time, I accepted things as they were and transitioned into my unhappily ever after.

I LEARNED THAT THERE WAS A WORLD OUTSIDE THE WORLD I SURVIVED IN. A WORLD WHERE ANYTHING MIGHT BE POSSIBLE.

NINE

THE GOOD, THE BAD, AND THE UGLY

WITH TESSIE gone, I was free to call Uncle John and Aunt Liza what their flesh and blood called them, and what I craved for so long—Mom and Pop. While this transition was a little awkward for Kat, for me it was like having an early Christmas present. Mom. Pop. Like honey it rolled off my tongue. Mom—a woman who nurtured me, instead of abusing me. Pop—the strength and reliability I never had in my life. Mom. Pop. Old enough to be my grandparents. Old enough to want to take it easy as they entered their golden years. Instead they signed up for ten more years of child rearing. Mom. Pop. And three older siblings.

Mom and Pop never offered to officially adopt Kat and me or give us their last name. While there were times when I wondered why they didn't take this extra step, it never bothered me because they were much more than my biological parents could ever be. They were the people who allowed me to dream of a better future and have a safer present. As far as I was concerned, I was their child.

While Mom and Pop were always there, it would be Anne who would spend the next ten years raising us. Bobby and Roger, already grown, had lives of their own. Nevertheless, they were there to teach me how to play basketball, let me hang out with them and their friends, take me to basketball games, and teach me the good, the bad, and the ugly of manhood.

Roger was an avid bowler. On occasional weekends he took me to Jersey Lanes in Linden to watch him bowl and play video games. The alley was filled with smoke and men drinking beer and having fun. It made me feel grown and accepted.

Bobby was more of an example of what not to be as a man. He and his first wife lived with Mom and Pop. On more than one occasion, I saw him beat and manhandle his wife. He was also cheating on her. When she could no longer take the abuse, she left him.

Once we arrived home from Tessie's funeral, Kat and I were half numb and half filled with anticipation for the future. Mom and Pop decided we needed an interruption from grieving before transitioning to the next chapter of our lives. One day as I walked past their bedroom, I saw Anne sitting on their bed surrounded by a pile of cash, talking to them in a hushed voice. Before I could ask what was going on, I was ushered out of the room and the door was shut behind me. A month later the five of us piled into the family van and left New Jersey. Only once we pulled into a motel parking lot in North Carolina, did Kat and I find out that we were going to Disney World.

Disney World! That was all we could think about from

THE GOOD, THE BAD, AND THE UGLY

that moment on. We were too excited to sleep. All night long it felt like our hearts would beat out of our tiny chests, picking up pace like a train rolling down a hill, each beat as the sound of train wheels ... Dis-ney World, Dis-ney World, Dis-ney World, Dis-ney World, Dis-ney World! From the slums of Savannah and the projects of New Jersey, Mutt and Jeff were Disney World bound!

The moment we pulled into Kissimmee, Florida, I was in love! In my entire life I had never seen such beauty and opulence. Manicured lawns with the brightest green grass I had ever seen, tall palm trees lining sides of clean streets, bright rooftops and pristine blue water swimming pools. The beauty of this place was emphasized at night when the lights came on. It felt like we were in an alternate reality altogether.

Each time we entered or left the resort premises we were greeted by staff who knew our names, as if we were lifelong friends or royalty. Kat and I took private tennis lessons while Anne and the parents watched us sponge up joy from every moment they gifted us. We spent our days exploring the Magic Kingdom, Universal Studios, Epcot Center, and MGM Studios. We even got to meet Mickey Mouse! In the evenings we frolicked in the pool, mingling with visitors from all over the United States while trying to avoid getting a brain freeze from slurping up too much ice cream.

There was no bedtime!

One night while the rest were sound asleep, I indulged in too much TV. Eleven years old, instead of gorging on cartoons, I got lost in watching the history of the resort where we stayed. My imagination soared. This was the night when I decided that I no longer had to live in fear of ending up a homeless man when I grew up (something that gave me anxiety and night sweats for many years prior). Being there broadened my horizons. I learned that there was a world outside the world I survived in for the last eleven years. A world where anything might be possible. With everyone asleep, my imagination ran wild and free. Could I create wealth instead of homelessness when I grew up? Could I even own a resort like this one if I put hard work into it? There was no one to stop me from dreaming.

Leaving Florida was bittersweet. I wanted the trip to last forever. I cried on the way back. Life in New Jersey seemed bleak and colorless compared to this new world I discovered. Over the next few years, as if hearing my silent prayers, the family brought us back to Disney World, the place where my thirst for a better life grew deeper and the seeds of desire to become something more than I was grew stronger. Eventually, I resolved that I would let nothing stop me from making it big in life.

Back home, we settled into our lives. Kat and I were enrolled at Victory Christian Academy, a private school. It seemed like the Browns spared no expense taking care of us. The school was a beautiful melting pot filled with Latinos, African Americans, Haitians, Poles, and Italians. Kat and I relaxed into being kids and made friends. We went to school and had a sense of normalcy.

Years of abuse and neglect had suppressed my true personality. In the shadows of my biological parents, I spent the first part of my life in survival mode. I felt too scared to push the boundaries to discover who I was and what it meant to be human. If I had loving parents who corrected, encouraged, and nurtured me, I could have grown into my identity and developed necessary social skills. With Tessie gone, I was now free to discover myself on my own. And what I discovered was surprising—I was not as shy as I thought, but had rather a boisterous and outgoing personality. And what better place to test the boundaries of how far I could take my newfound self than at school?

Traditional education methods did not take into account my years of neglect and stunted development. They certainly did not accommodate my hyper, ever-moving body and mind. I was not meant to sit behind a desk to learn. But it would be years before breakthroughs in education would happen to accommodate varied learning styles. Meanwhile, I found it hard to concentrate and listen. And teachers found it hard to keep me interested and learning.

When they could not fit a square peg into a round hole, the school administration placed me into a special ed class. I can tell you that there was nothing special about special ed. In my experience, special education was a broken system, staffed with teachers who were incapable of meeting the demands of children with diverse learning abilities. The only thing that special ed succeeded at, besides giving me the stigma of being dumb, was further failing me in academics.

I was determined that I would not become invisible. So what I lacked in academics, I made up for with my personality. I became the class clown, which frequently got me in trouble.

While I was settling into my school and social life, Kat's and my life took a turn toward a very familiar place—a street where love and hate, discipline and abuse commingle so much that they become hard to tell apart. They fuse into a monster that chases you even in your dreams, stealing your very breath. A monster that you try to love, because it is the only creature you know. A monster that causes you to develop a Stockholm syndrome and defend your abusers.

With Mom and Pop aging, our discipline fell into Anne's hands. Only sixteen years my senior, then in her twenties, she was still figuring out her life and knew very little of what to do with children like us. Ironically, she had a degree in Early Childhood Education and was destined to work with youngsters for years to come.

Before I knew it, I was back at the mercy of yet another woman who was supposed to love me, yet at times, took me to a point of unconsciousness. Any minor mishap and I would be beaten with anything she could grab.

A wooden paddle that was a couple of inches thick and a couple of feet long was one of her favorites. More than once, she would have me strip naked, spread myself on the bed in a Superman pose, forbidden to move. The paddle coming down hard on my exposed young body. Wham! It hurt like hell. I lost my breath. She watched me. Waited until I began to breathe again. Wham! Smack! Wham! My body shivering from pain, cold in the anticipation of the next blow. Helpless and ashamed, stripped of my humanity, tears streaming down my face. Is this what all women are like? Is this what love is?

Once, when she was done with the beating, I dared to get up, every cell of my body burning from pain. She extended the paddle, stuck it under my penis, shoved it up, and moved it around, as if stirring a pot. "Hmmm ... " she said and exited the room. Violated, humiliated, and crushed, I was too afraid to think what my future would be like. There was nowhere to turn this time. No other Brown family to escape to.

Anne was young. Where could she have learned such cruelty? Could it have been that this is how she and her siblings were raised? Could it have been the norm in the African American community, as I often observed? Could it be something that our people learned from their White masters during slavery and passed it down for generations,

THE GOOD, THE BAD, AND THE UGLY

justifying hate by calling it discipline? Where could so much viciousness come from and how could all of it fit into one human being? Into a family who promised to love and protect us?

Familiarity breeds contempt, the saying goes. In my case, familiarity bred abuse. Kat and I traded hell for heaven when we left Tessie, only to find ourselves back where we started. The transition time was a world of illusion we created in our suffering minds.

As time passed, Anne explored all methods of torture. Paddles, extension cords, two-by-fours, her hands, wire hangers, metal spoons, sticks, switches, and shoes. She also used mental torture. Short of waterboarding, my punishments had all the makings of Guantanamo Bay. I was to be subdued for any mishap, misunderstanding, or act of disobedience. Not doing my chores, standing up for myself at school, even rocking myself to sleep—anything could set her off.

When I felt scared at night, I would sneak into Kat's bed—this is how we protected and comforted each other when living with Tessie. However, if Anne caught me in Kat's bed, I would be awakened by a loud slap on my face. There was no rhyme or reason as to why this, or anything else, I did would upset her, leaving me petrified to do anything that would provoke her wrath.

I was around eight years old when Kat and I visited Anne in college, and I must have done something to upset her. Anne's temper flared. She wanted to subdue me. To put the fear of God in me, she told Kat to stand by the phone and be prepared to dial 9-1-1 because I would need medical attention after she was done beating me.

She told me to get inside her room, strip down, and get ready. Instead, scared, I took off running down the hall of her dormitory, making enough noise for the neighbors to hear my desperate cry. Struggling to catch up, she finally had me in her arms, begging me to stop screaming. Once I saw her next-door neighbor peek out of his room, I felt safe enough to calm down. That day I lived to avoid a whipping, but I was not so fortunate other days.

Where Anne's physical abuse stopped, humiliation took over as its ugly twin. The pain I experienced was always compounded by humiliation.

Liza and John were of old beliefs when it came to personal hygiene. Not modern-day Americans who love to shower once or twice a day, the Browns were frugal when it came to water usage. We did not get to flush the toilet after each time we used it—bodily discharge accumulated until Mom or Pop would decide it could be flushed. Showering and bathing was a luxury. If we bathed, Kat and I bathed in the same water. Instead of showering, we washed ourselves out of the sink with washcloths the best we could, not always doing a great job.

When I was about nine, my teacher, Mrs. Rodriguez, pulled me out of class and rushed me to the principal's office. Mr. DeMarco, a dark-haired Italian in his mid-forties, six-foot-two, towered over me as we entered his office. His eyes burrowed into my face with an unkind glare. This man was known for his bad temper and abrasiveness. Mrs. Rodriguez whispered something in his ear. He glared at me. I felt scared. Walking over, he grabbed my sweater, sniffed me and shoved me aside.

"You stink," he said abruptly.

I was so embarrassed, I wanted the floor to open and swallow me alive.

They dialed Liza to let her know they were sending me home to shower, put on deodorant, change, and come back to school.

As we left Mr. DeMarco's office, Mrs. Rodriguez was noticeably unsettled.

"I'm sorry, Demetrye," she said. "You didn't do anything wrong. I just can't take the smell." Her apology did not make me feel any better. I felt embarrassed and ashamed. It felt like the entire school was watching me as Mrs. Rodriguez walked me to the front of the school to get picked up.

Aunt Liza seemed bothered when she came to get me. I was too humiliated to say anything, so we stayed quiet the entire ride home. Showered and with a fresh outfit on, I returned to school to finish the day.

Embarrassment aside, I was a good-looking boy. Girls paid attention to me. However, I was forbidden to date. In fact, I was forbidden to do most anything outside of school and church. Mom's favorite response to any of my requests was "No!" Going to the park, having friends over, going over to a friend's house, calling a classmate, going to the backyard, or even sitting on the front porch—the answer was always "No."

There were times when I would still feel hungry after a meal.

"Mom, can I have more food, please?" I would ask.

"No. You just had a meal," Aunt Liza would reply.

Hungry, I had to wait for the next meal. If I were lucky, however, I would find old cans of applesauce, sneak them into my closet, use a nail and a shoe to punch holes in them and drink their contents to fill my hungry belly.

Dating was strictly forbidden. However, as we all know, there is nothing sweeter than the forbidden fruit. Damn the consequences! At fourteen, I decided to throw caution to the wind and secretly date a cute Puerto Rican girl named Jessica. It took only a few weeks before Anne found out. When she did, humiliation found my address.

I was awakened by Anne in the wee morning hours. "Dee, get up, get dressed, and let's go!"

Barely awake, I dragged myself for ten blocks behind her, beginning to understand with each step where I was being led like a lamb to the slaughter. Anne was taking me to Jessica's house. She knew! My heart felt like it was about to leap out of my chest and die. Beads of cold sweat collecting on my forehead. I was awash with anxiety, praying that her wrath would not be poured out on me in front of the girl I adored. "What would Jessica think? What would she say about me at school?" were thoughts running through my mind.

When we arrived, Anne sat me on the bench across the street from Jessica's house.

"Dee, whose house is it? Who lives here? Who is this girl? How long have you been talking to her?"

Her questions kept coming like a tidal wave. Her voice was eerily calm, but I knew it was the calm before the storm. It was not out of the realm of possibility that she would knock on Jessica's door. I would have died a thousand deaths if that were to happen.

Forty minutes later, escaping death by humiliation, she marched me back home. As soon as we hit the front door, all my stylish clothes were confiscated. She knew me well enough to strike where it hurt: my pride. For the next two weeks I would be forced to wear old clothes to school. To be seen in out-of-style clothes by my classmates, and worst of all by Jessica, was mortifying. If academics was not my strength, looking fly was. I had style and got respect for it. Anne stripped me of that. But my punishment did not end there. Making me stand next to her on our arrival home, Anne dialed Jessica's mom.

THE GOOD, THE BAD, AND THE UGLY

"Dee is not allowed to date, Ms. Lopez. We do not allow dating in our household. Dee and Jessica must break up."

The blood drained out of my face. What would Jessica think? What would she tell our classmates? I was mortified. It took me a few days to work up the courage to break up with Jessica at school.

My romantic life was dead before having a chance to blossom. Jessica and I would not speak again for at least two years, and it would take another year before I would give secret dating another chance.

As I was growing up, my punishments remained much the same. A young man, I felt like a helpless boy still. Fifteen years old, I would still be put in time outs like a toddler. On more than one occasion, in frustration, Anne would make me sit on a chair, forbidding me to move.

"Sit here. Don't move. If you move, I will beat you," she would threaten.

And I sat there, scared to move. Two, three hours at a time.

While living with Tessie, I developed a self-soothing habit of rocking myself to sleep. On the bed, under my sheets, side to side, rhythmically moving until my tired body would feel safe enough to doze off. This habit stayed with me well into my college years. But if Anne ever caught me rocking, she would hit me and demand that I stop.

"It is stupid, Dee," she would tell me. "So, stop it! Just stop!"

To make me stop, she would tuck me in so tight that I could barely move under the sheets.

I was a prisoner in their home, confined to their will. The place that once provided me with safety from Tessie's wrath became my prison.

I spent the rest of my time living with the Browns walking on eggshells. Always expecting to be denied one thing or another, or punished at the slightest provocation or without any at all.

Pain and pleasure, love and violence blurred into an indiscernible pattern. For nineteen years of my life, until the day I would leave for college, I felt that they always existed together. So when I was challenged by someone outside my community about Browns' methods of discipline, I felt like I had to defend and justify them. After all, wasn't this how families showed love?

Humiliation and physical abuse were mingled with manipulation. Beatings were often mixed with "I love you, that's why I am doing this," as well as being embraced right after. Sometimes I would receive gifts after my body had been covered with bruises so big and painful that I had to skip school so no one would discover my reality. Beatings so severe that I could not bend my elbow or would walk with a limp for days. Attacks so vicious that Anne would have to take breaks between strikes. She would be so blinded by anger and rage that more than once, Pop would have to come into the room to stop her.

While Anne was busy in her role as the physical disciplinarian, Mom and Pop were hands off. Perhaps too tired from raising their own children, they did not beat me. I barely got spanked by Mom. She was the antidote to Anne's violence, although she never stopped her. Pop lashed out only on occasion. Only once do I remember him beating me senseless until Bobby's wife stepped in to rescue me.

Pop's abuse came in a different form. It was mental. He called me stupid more times than I can remember, and he implied it even more frequently. I began to believe it and live up to it. By the age of nineteen, I had never heard him say "I love you" to me, but "What are you, stupid?" was something I was used to hearing.

I got accustomed to this life, like a frog in an urban myth

THE GOOD, THE BAD, AND THE UGLY

that gets used to hot water and would never jump out of it if it is slowly heated, remaining in it until it boils to death. So I too grew to think it was okay to whip a child senseless as long as he was shown a semblance of love afterward. In the world of psychology, this is called trauma bonding. Trauma bonding occurs as the result of ongoing cycles of abuse in which the intermittent reinforcement of reward and punishment creates powerful emotional bonds that are resistant to change. It is no wonder that, on average, it takes a victim of abuse seven attempts to leave an abuser before they escape for good. Somewhere along the way you begin to think that the abuse is your fault and you deserve it. It is all that you are good for, so you accept it and conform.

You lose yourself in the process. Self-esteem is gone. Zest for life is gone. You are broken. You can now be controlled. You float along purposeless, having a hard time forming lasting, loving, meaningful relationships.

I was no angel. I knew that. I came from abuse and brought my share of youthful dysfunction to the table, but I was willing to do anything to be loved, nurtured, and accepted. Anything! With some care and love, God knows, even the most troubled kids can turn into something great. I know that I would have responded better to love than to abuse. Instead, I began to feel like a prisoner inside a gilded cage I could not wait to escape.

Years later, when I could discern wholeness from dysfunction and discipline from abuse, I realized that the early warning signs of who the Browns truly were, were always there. In the beginning, I romanticized my life with them so much for what they had done for me, I overlooked a lot of things. Or, perhaps, I justified what I experienced thinking that this is what all families were like. Edward, Tessie, the Browns—for all I knew, this is what real love was supposed to feel like. And frankly, in my early years with them anything seemed better than living with Tessie.

The love the Browns offered became my curse. It followed me into my adulthood, destroying everything in its path.

I WAS IN DENIAL
THAT WHAT WAS
HAPPENING
TO ME AND MY
SISTER WAS NOT
NORMAL.

TEN

WITHOUT A TRACE

Dysfunctional as it may seem, I was favored by Anne and the Browns. Meanwhile, Kat never found her place in their family. She would spend the rest of her time living with them feeling like second-hand goods. An outcast. She was Esau to my Jacob. Whether it was her feisty personality, her sneaking boys into the room at night to have their way with her, or the fact that she looked a lot like Tessie, the Browns treated her less favorably than me.

Kat got whipped, but she was fearless. This was one of the things I admired most about her. I was always afraid to get into trouble because I was afraid of the beatings I would get; not Kat, she stood her ground. She did not care about repercussions. Only a year and a half older than me, she felt it was her responsibility to look out for me. She never allowed anyone to bully me in school or at home. When I was still young and felt defenseless, I kept quiet when we were mistreated; she spoke up for both of us. This did not create much favor for her with the Browns.

On more than one occasion, Kat stood up to Anne. One time, when she did, Anne slapped her on her face. Kat slapped her back. The battle of the fists then turned into the battle of the words—Anne told Kat that she wasn't going to amount to anything in life and was only good for lying on her back just like her mother. Kat did not let up. She lived to speak her mind. Feeling powerless and fed up, Anne threatened to contact our family in South Carolina to have them come get Kat. Kat only relished in the threat.

"Bring it on!" she roared at Anne.

Even days later, Kat was still stoking the fire: "Have you called the Grants yet, Anne?" she prodded. "When are they coming to pick me up?"

Kat's mistreatment did not stop at Anne. While Aunt Liza stayed away from physical punishments, she was a master of mental torture. She suffered from hemorrhoids and on more than one occasion, when Kat misbehaved, she would take her to the bathroom to show her blood in the toilet. She would tell her it was Kat's disobedience causing her to suffer like this. Kat's inner world was crumbling to pieces—she began to believe that she was the cause of Aunt Liza's suffering, but at the same time rage was filling her young heart. How could a grown person put such a burden on her shoulders? What was she supposed to do with such guilt? The cross in this case was indeed too heavy to bear.

While I lived to pacify Anne's wrath and chose to submit to the Browns' way of life, Kat was the challenger. She spoke her mind even if it meant punishment, rejection, and isolation. Broken and wounded. Always the rebel. Feisty as hell. My soul's twin, she yearned for love just as I did, but she had to survive without it. They made her life harder than mine. It would take me years to learn about just how badly she suffered and how far their cruelty went.

The entire Brown family were churchgoers. One Sunday afternoon, after the morning service, I found myself witnessing Roger rape my sister ... in the kitchen of the church. At the time, I did not know what to call what I saw. All I knew was that I was horrified witnessing it, but I did not know who to turn to for help. Years later, as an adult, I worked up the courage to talk to Kat about it. She told me that it was not an isolated incident. She said she knew asking for help would only get her into more trouble because the Browns resented her so much. They would not consider her as trustworthy as their beloved son. She knew that they would not protect her innocence. So she kept quiet.

At some point Kat shut down and never came back. When beatings and abuse no longer worked, the Browns' go-to discipline method was threatening to kick her out. They did it often, and as I would soon learn, they meant it.

One day, she pushed their patience just a bit too far. Firmly forbidden to go to her high school prom by our very strict Christian benefactors, Kat decided to throw caution to the wind. Damn the consequences—she went. This was the last day Kat called the Browns' home her own. Later that night, when she called to let Mom know she was on her way, Aunt Liza told her that she had no home to come back to. Her bags were packed and left on the front porch. At the age of seventeen, still a child, Kat found herself homeless like a stray dog.

I was not home when this happened. When I got back the day after, I was told that Kat left because she refused to follow the household rules. Leaving was her idea. Young and naïve, I believed them.

Kat vanished, and I did not know where to go looking for her. She disappeared not only from our house, but also from my life. She was to be erased from my existence—Anne even cut her out of family photos. Mutt and Jeff were to be separated for good this time.

Nearly two years would pass before I would see her again, that time with a beautiful child in her arms—my niece. A quick conversation, a hug and a kiss, and my sister disappeared again. Disappearing became her specialty, just like it was Tessie's. For years Kat would only be found when she wanted to be. Years would pass before we would reconnect and I would learn the truth of her exile.

In time, Kat told me that much like me, she felt like she was living in a prison at the Browns. All she wanted to do was escape the physical and psychological abuse. Albeit too young to be on her own when she got kicked out, Kat knew one thing—she had to make it and would figure it out because she wanted to be free. Free from abuse. Free from control. Free to be the person she was born to be. None of which could have been achieved if she stayed locked up in our gilded prison.

While I was too naïve to see reality for what it was, my tender feisty sister saw the Browns for who they were. When I was growing up, even considering the abuse they subjected me to, compared to Tessie they were angels to me. I had a roof over my head, food to eat and was surrounded by people who loved me. Even though I would get beat, this was still heaven to me. This family took me in as their own and gave me the best life I thought was possible.

At that time, I was young and in need of love and a home so much that I was blind to seeing what was in front of me. I was in denial that what was happening to me and my sister was not normal. All I knew then was that this is how the

Black community raised and loved their young. But I was not to remain ignorant for much longer. Soon enough, I too would start seeing reality for what it was.

IT WAS NOT GOD OR THE CHURCH THAT WOULD FINALLY GET MY ATTENTION AND PROVIDE ME A TURNING POINT.

ELEVEN

TURNING POINT

A CAGED bird never feels fully alive. It needs space to stretch its wings. It needs flight to taste freedom. Otherwise it will never thrive.

With Kat's disappearance, I needed to find out who I was. When she left and I didn't know why, I was mad. I felt betrayed. I felt that a part of me was missing. For fifteen years we had been inseparable. And now I was all alone. Mutt and Jeff no more. So I began to push boundaries. Smoking weed, secretly dating, getting into fights at school, even stealing money from the school administrative office, and on one occasion, even from Mom.

Once unleashed, the rebel in me was hard to stop. I was kicked out of the private school. Anne no longer knew what to do. Beatings no longer had the same effect on me. I would put up with them, but still do my thing. Much like Kat, I wanted freedom. At her wit's ends and feeling powerless,

Anne took me to Rahway prison to scare me straight.

Established in the 1970s, Scared Straight programs were and still are being used as a tool to deter juvenile crime. They usually entail visits by at-risk youth to adult prisons where they hear about the harsh realities of prison life from inmates.

While programs like these are created by people with well-meaning intentions, I believe their effects on a young mind can be damaging. Statistically, most of these programs fail. In my case, however, scared straight is what I got ... at least for a while. I was scared straight the moment I arrived at the facility. The rest of my stay was an added bonus.

There were fifteen of us out-of-control teens. We stood by the gate, huddled together, waiting for it to open. Before long the inmates began catcalling us. I was terrified. I was too young and pretty for this place.

Finally, security walked us into a gymnasium where we were greeted by a group of inmates handpicked to speak to us. Mincing no words, they spoke to us candidly, explicitly, and vulgarly. These men were not put away for white collar crimes. These were rapists, drug dealers, and murderers. Thrown into the prison system, a threat to society, these men found it somewhere in their hearts to care enough to give us their time. They did not want us to become them.

After the candid conversation, we were taken to cell blocks. Lined up in a straight line, we shuffled along.

"I heard you like to sneak out at night to visit your girlfriend," said a raspy deep voice right into my ear.

Turning around, I was nose-to-nose with a burly Black man. Covered in tattoos, staring down into my soul, he made a chilling promise: "Disobey your sister one more time and I will kick your punk ass!"

Disconnected from reality, for a moment I forgot that it

would be impossible for him to carry out this threat with me being on the outside. I nodded my head in agreement.

"Yes, I understand," I muttered.

I was scared straight ... but not for long. After my initial experience the fear wore off. As the saying goes, "out of sight, out of mind." Before long I was back to smoking weed. (Alcohol was never my vice. It might have been Aunt Liza's fire and brimstone sermons that drunkards would spend eternity in hell being rooted deep in my mind, but I never thirsted after a bottle.)

Anne was at her wit's end. Beatings were no longer working and Scared Straight had failed. The only thing left was religion.

I was required to attend church as often as possible, sometimes spending up to four days a week at services. While I was pushing certain boundaries, I wasn't willing to go to the same extremes as Kat and lose my family, so I complied. I was taken to several churches to keep me out of trouble, but as irony would have it, it was not God or the church that would finally get my attention and provide me a turning point.

One evening, on the way home from dropping off a friend, Anne and I witnessed a cold-blooded murder. There were four teenagers on the side of the street. As we drove off, I looked in the rearview mirror and saw one of them pull out a gun and shoot another in the face. I was shocked. The other three scattered as the victim slid down on the pavement, his body hitting a black SUV parked nearby.

"Anne! I just saw someone get shot!"

Anne floored the gas pedal and we remained silent the rest of the ride home. We reported the murder promptly on arrival.

This was my turning point. My world was rocked. I realized that if I continued on the path I was forging, my life would end up one of two ways—in prison or dead. Instead of pushing boundaries to find myself, I needed to find a purpose. If I were killed, God forbid, I was too afraid of hell to die unrepented. Growing up I spent the majority of my life hearing about the wrath of God. The fear of hell was too real to ignore any longer. So at the impressionable age of seventeen I got saved and found purpose.

I traded weed for Bible reading, sneaking around for reading theology books, and started going to church of my own accord rather than being delivered to one like a prisoner against his will. My time was now dedicated to prayer, fasting, and searching for ways to hear the divine voice. Rather than feeling like a caged bird, I now found solace in my room, often lost in prayer and worship. I sought out youth who, like me, had a taste for eternity and wanted to dedicate their lives in the pursuit of it.

I was still whipped for stepping out of line, but these events were fewer and farther between. Anne and the parents felt that their prayers were finally answered. The prodigal son had come home. Their enthusiasm for my born-again experience manifested in a constant supply of Christian literature, books, and tapes, many of which centered on the teachings of hell and the retribution of sin.

My memories of Tessie were fading. Because of my religious indoctrination, I was fearfully certain that I would never see her again. Unless she repented on her deathbed, I was sure she would spend eternity in hell. She was a disgrace of a mother and a human being. I pushed her out of my mind to the point she became a ghost and slipped away into the deepest vault of my awareness.

About a year before I graduated from high school, we learned that Anne had cancer. Only in her thirties, we were

TURNING POINT

all devastated. As she entered this season of fighting for her life, we focused on supporting her. Despite everything I endured, I loved her. She was my family and that was enough to give her all the support I could muster.

I entered a year of peace and calm. I was still a straight D and F student, but now I was a working man. Between school, church, work, and Anne's health condition, I was too busy to sin. Anne was focused on her health so there was no more fear of physical punishment.

Within a year, after multiple treatments and a radical hysterectomy, Anne's life was saved. We were certain it was because of our prayers. This lit up my spiritual thirst even more. Having witnessed a miracle, I knew I had to serve the god who saved her.

My high school graduation was fast approaching, and I now was thinking about the next phase of my life. I found my life's calling—I wanted to be a preacher. I wanted to save others from the same pain and wretchedness I lived under most of my life. I wanted to spread the news of God's goodness. Even though my caregivers weren't the greatest examples of love, I met many people who became my role models of what God's love should feel like. I also began to discover God for myself, which made me want to share him with others even more.

Graduating from high school in 1998, I was admitted into a Bible college. The rest of my life was staring me right in the face, teasing with possibilities, but silent about the highs and the lows I would experience over the next few years, telling me nothing about how, one day, I would find my true salvation and freedom.

A TORTURE CYCLE
OF PLEASURE AND
GUILT ENVELOPED
ME DAILY.

TWELVE

FORBIDDEN FRUIT

I RECEIVED admission into college at the last minute. I had three days to pack, get on the Greyhound bus, and make my way to Columbus, Ohio. Like a caged bird learning to fly for the first time, I felt like my chest could finally expand wide enough for me to take a deep breath and take flight.

As Anne drove me away from the house, I looked back to bid farewell. I knew that I would never call Linden my home again. I had only a suitcase and a few hundred dollars to my name, but that was all I needed. I was in a hurry to be free.

By the time I arrived, the college dorms were already filled. I had no place to stay, but I was determined to claim my independence. There was no going back! I was going to figure it out. For the first time in my life, I would be allowed to be a man. And a man I became.

That very day I found an apartment and two roommates to share it with. The three of us had the same goal for being there—to uncover the will of God and to experience life for ourselves. I was excited. A job followed shortly after. Free at last! Free at last! Thank God Almighty, I was free at last!

The experience of being on my own was invigorating. I had no one to answer to. I was my own man and it felt great. I was free from the Browns and their hold on my life. I was a reborn born-again man surrounded by like-minded people. Holiness and God's calling were my destiny.

I submerged myself in my education, majoring in pastoral studies. In the beginning, my academic performance lagged as it did in the past. But with time, I found my stride and became an honor roll student.

My extrovert personality blossomed. Before long, my apartment was the hub of noisy get togethers, parties, and Bible studies. I participated in every possible activity I could—volunteering my time at the prayer lines of the mega church I attended, serving as a security guard at large events, and helping the less fortunate on my days off. I could stay out as late as I wanted, make friends with whoever I wanted, and call the shots for the first time in my life. There was no one to tell me "No." I was recognized and respected. I felt like I had finally found my place in life. Not a dark cloud in the sky. My cup was overflowing ...

Until my past came to visit me.

It seemed like being in a new place, having a new life, and praying until my tongue went numb was not enough to escape what resided deep within me. The dark seed sown by Edward and Tessie had become a tree whose deep roots invaded every crevice of my subconscious mind.

Raised by a whore, I learned early in life how to pleasure myself. While I had not yet had sex with a woman, I was acquainted with masturbation all too well. Though no longer a taboo in larger society, being a boy from a Christian home and a man who was now attending a seminary, I would be damned by God and my own self-loathing for drawing pleasure from my fleshly garden. Busy being in love with my new faith, my soul had only a few short months of respite. As I caved to my carnal habits, my insecurities and shame came back with a vengeance.

The pleasure-shame-repentance cycle continued for years. I could not shake who I was despite prayer and fasting. I could not live with the guilt and longed to place the blame on someone else. Tessie was it. Had it not been for her, I thought, I would have never discovered the forbidden fruit, never partaken of it, and never felt this shame. She became my scapegoat, and no longer the woman whose love and approval I craved. She was now the enemy. A mere vessel God used to bring me into this world.

Within a year of my newfound freedom and playing hide-and-seek with my old self, I became friends with a group of young women who attended the same college and lived in my apartment complex. They were easygoing and great company, like sisters I never had. One of them, a fair-skinned brunette Californian, captured my heart. Laid back, pretty, bubbly, kind, smart, easy to talk to—Tracy made my heart skip a beat. Slowly our friendship turned into dating. I thought I was in love. So much so that I gave Tracy a promise ring.

At first our relationship was pure and innocent, conforming to the religious expectations around us. Then, with no watchful eye over us (and my curiosity and desires stronger than my beliefs), we took it to a place of no return.

I thought I had died and gone to heaven. Self-pleasure was no rival to this exhilarating, earth-shattering, roar-of-thunder-in-your-heart physical experience with a woman. Nothing I had ever tried could ever compare to it. It was the forbidden fruit I knew I should not have tasted, but it tasted so good!

I was not meant to dwell in that heavenly realm of pleasure for long, however. Soon I plunged into the bottomless crevices of hell. Observing what Tessie did throughout my childhood and raised by the Browns who never spoke about it, I had a very distorted view of sex. Shame, guilt, self-loathing—the unholy trinity came rushing in. I was repentant. But as any man with red blood coursing through his veins knows, once you've tasted the forbidden fruit, once you've released your stallion, it's next to impossible to bring it back under control. A man's nature is a wild horse that does not like to be bridled. Mine was no exception.

For the next two months I rode the roller coaster of heaven and hell, pleasure and condemnation. An exemplary Bible student by day, writing sermons, preaching and spitting fire, sharing the love of God with others; by night, a shameful, sneaking-around-and-loving-every-single-moment-of-it fornicator. I was lost in Tracy and she was lost in me. We both looked for opportunities to steal joy that did not seem to belong to us. However, retribution for our indulgence was just around the corner.

One snowy winter morning I received a call that brought our budding love affair to a screeching halt.

"Demetrye, you need to come over," she said. "We need to talk."

"What is it, Tracy? Can you tell me?" My heart dropped into my gut.

"No. You have to come over."

Moments later we met in her car outside our apartment building.

"I'm pregnant," she said, fighting back tears.

"You're what?" I felt like I was hit by a freight train. I

could not think straight. My world turned upside down. I froze. Only my thoughts racing. The affair we could hide. The guilt I could live with. But a pregnancy? The whole world would know! We would be expelled from the college. Sex outside of marriage went against the code of conduct the school had in place. I would lose my friends. And my family? My family would kill me. I was only twenty years old, still trying to figure out how to be a man. How could I be a father? What could I do?!

"Demetrye. Demetrye! Say something!" She was looking at me for answers.

Holding on to the door of the car, I steadied myself, looking for something to snap me back into reality.

"Well ... I am here to support you in whatever you want to do," I said, my head still spinning.

"What?! You want me to have an abortion? I will not have an abortion!" She charged at me.

"No! That's not what I meant, Tracy!" I responded. "I am here to support you through everything. I will do my part. I will pitch in for the medical bills. I will learn what to do to be a father. We got this."

As she exhaled, relieved yet still very much scared, she shared her fears with me.

"Demetrye, people will talk. They will see my body change. They will judge me. You are not the one they will point their fingers at. They will see ME."

"Then it looks like you and I need to have a conversation with the college administration," I offered. "It's better they learn the truth from us."

So, we did. We met with Mr. Carpenter, one of the college instructors, to share our news.

"We used to recommend for couples to get married in situations like yours," he said, after listening to our confession. Apparently, we were not the only God-seeking youngsters tempted by the flesh. "With time, however, we learned that it was not the best solution. So, it's up to you to decide what you want to do. In the meantime, avoid physical intimacy. And ... you are suspended from college."

Suspended or not, we both felt relieved. We no longer needed to keep this secret hidden. The truth was out, and now we needed to deal with the future.

I was twenty. She was three years my senior. Young, and now totally devastated, we were committed to making it work. Marriage was what we decided on. I thought our child deserved both parents. While I never knew the love of a parent, I was willing to move heaven and hell to learn how to become a devoted father.

We began to plan our future, although it did not look promising. While not as dysfunctional as me, Tracy came from a broken home. Her parents were divorced. Tracy's childhood was cut short because she had to become a parent, taking care of her mother's emotional and physical needs. However, what she lacked at home she made up for in her social life. This California girl knew how to party and have fun. Ours was not her first love affair.

The more I got to know Tracy, the more I realized that we did not have much in common. We could not agree on anything. I wanted to live in Florida after graduation. She wanted to move back to California. I wanted to become a pastor. She loathed the idea. It seemed that the only common interest she and I would have in our marriage would be our child.

I was too young and naïve to be honest with myself, so I pushed aside my doubts and concerns. Instead of pursuing happiness, I put my responsibilities first. I was focused on preparing to become a good father, happiness be damned.

With seminary studies ending, I submerged myself in studying books on parenting.

In a matter of weeks, medical bills began to pour in faster than I could earn money. Tracy was experiencing health complications and had frequent doctor visits. Neither of us had health insurance. At first, I paid the bills as soon as Tracy handed them to me, making me responsible for every single penny. But it wasn't long before I was way over my head and could not keep up with my monthly expenses and stay on top of the bills. Finally, as I leafed through the subsequent batch of statements, I had to speak up.

Dialing her number, my stomach churning, feeling less than the man I wanted to be, I said, "Tracy, I simply cannot keep paying all these bills on my own."

"What do you mean you can't? You told me you would take care of this!" she snapped.

"Yes, I told you I would contribute whatever I possibly could, Tracy. But, given the circumstances, it's gonna have to take both of us to keep up with these bills."

This moment became the defining moment in our relationship. She turned into a person I could not recognize. Screaming, she came at me.

"What are you saying? Are you saying that you're done? You had fun and now you are leaving me?"

"No. I am not leaving. What I am telling you is that we both have to take responsibility."

After a few more explosive exchanges between us, something I was not emotionally trained to handle, I hung up the phone and went to get some air. I wanted to be the man who paid all of the bills. A man who takes care of his responsibilities. But I was too young and too broke to take care of it all on my own. It was hard, but I had to acknowledge that since there were two of us who got into this situation, it should be the two of us working together to take care of the bills as well.

When I got back, I learned that she had stopped by, crying and looking for me. Still upset, I decided to take the night to cool off. The next day, I went by her apartment, bringing a portion of the bills with me. She wasn't home, so I left them with her roommate.

I did not hear from Tracy again. Too stubborn and immature in handling emotional conflict, I waited for her to reach out. It seemed that she was waiting for the same.

A couple of weeks later I received a call from Mr. Carpenter.

"Demetrye, Tracy had a miscarriage."

An emotional tornado hit my gut. Dysfunctional as our situation was, I wanted this baby. I was prepared to become the father I never had. I had already planned our future. Grief washed over me. For years to come I would wonder what my baby would have looked and sounded like. Would it have been a boy or a girl? Would she have had my chocolate brown or Tracy's ocean blue eyes? What games would we have played together? I was grief stricken, as I am sure Tracy was too.

Raised by emotionally constipated people, I did not know what to do. I was hoping she would reach out if she needed me. I felt too paralyzed to take the first step. I assumed that she would not want to speak to me after our first and only argument. In my fear, I abandoned her in her greatest hour of need—a regret that would stay with me for years. If I could turn back time, I would have handled the situation differently.

Yet at the same time, I felt relieved. Relieved that our lives would not be bound together forever. Relieved that I would have a chance to grow up and make life-altering decisions rationally, rather than as an effort to cover up my transgressions.

I went on avoiding her and she avoided me. Months would pass by before we crossed paths at the church we both attended.

"Hi, Tracy," I said. "How are you doing?"

"Fine," was her only response as she passed by.

Just like that, my first adult relationship was over. However, there was still a price to pay for my youthful indiscretions.

Tracy and I had to sit out a year of college, getting our lives back in order. I was focused on working through the mess we created and getting back to my calling. Focused on salvaging my relationship with God, I was totally unaware about the cataclysm that was headed my way. As I was about to reenter college, one day my roommate came home bewildered.

"Demetrye, is it true?" he asked.

"What's true, Jeremy?"

"Is it true that you raped Tracy?" he asked in a ghastly voice.

"What? Why would you say that?!" I could barely breathe. Why would he ask me such a question?

"I was just at a party where it was implied," he responded. "Is it true, Demetrye?"

"Of course not! You should know me better. We've been like brothers for the last year and a half. Don't you know me, Jeremy?"

Word spread like wildfire—Demetrye the rapist.

I was many things, but this ... this I was not! This would not do! I already spent nineteen years of my life living in hell. I could not allow my life to turn to ruins now. I had to get out in front of this train wreck before it devastated my entire life.

Two days later I met Tracy at the administrative office. Truth had to be told and heard. We met with Mr. Parson.

"What's going on, guys?"

"I'm hearing that Tracy is telling people that I raped her, Mr. Parson. I am here to have her tell the truth," I responded.

Turning to Tracy, Mr. Parson asked, "Did he, Tracy?"

"Yes," she answered unyieldingly.

"When?" My body contorted under the pain of her accusation and betrayal. "The first, second, third, or the sixth time we slept together?" I asked.

Nothing. Silence.

"How about we see Mr. Carpenter? He has the recording of our conversation." I asked.

"No. No need for that," Mr. Parson replied, apparently already aware of our situation. "Here is what you two should do—talk it over, patch it up, and move on with your lives."

That was the last time Tracy and I would ever speak to each other. We attended the same college, the same church, crossed each other's paths, but never a word exchanged between us again.

Hell hath no fury like a woman scorned was the lesson I learned. Could it be that she was bothered by me not paying all the medical bills? Or hurt that I did not reach out in my naïveté when she had a miscarriage? This is something I will never know. But what I did know in the winter of 2001 was that I was done with women. It seemed that they were all placed on this planet to hurt me and I was done allowing that to happen.

Fate would have it differently soon enough. But in the meantime, shrouded in shame, guilt, self-loathing, and the pain of betrayal by my friends who were whispering behind my back, I wanted to move on with my life. However, my mother's legacy, which was deeply ingrained in my soul, sprouted yet another branch. I set on the path of destruction by night, while waging a war for my soul by day.

My decision to be done with women was fueled by anger and pain, forcing me to repress my sexual desires until I expressed them in destructive ways. Pornography, strip clubs, blow jobs—the devil's claws were sinking into my soul faster than I could repent for my transgressions. A torture cycle of pleasure and guilt enveloping me daily. Freed on Sunday, while spending all day in church, I sank to the bottom of hell's infinite pit during the week in the secret of my night life. Each time I sank a little deeper. Each time was a little more secretive. Each time I felt more ashamed.

From the depth of my tormented soul, daily I cried out to God, begging for salvation. Prayer, fasting, laying on of hands, repentance—nothing could help stop me from speeding down the spiral to self-destruction.

Nothing could cast this devil out. He became my master as my soul entered its darkest hours. It would take a miracle to pry me out of the grip of hell. A miracle that would break through as a small ray of light, piercing through my darkness. Gently. Firmly. Unintentionally. Persistently. Until it would flood my being with its salvation.

A miracle that would show up in the very form I wanted to reject the most—a woman. A green-eyed, hourglass-shaped, no-nonsense, charismatic Russian brunette. She was to save my life at the cost of her own. She just didn't know it yet. And neither did I, otherwise I would have pushed her away to spare her.

PART THREE

TRUE LOVE

IN TRUTH, I HAD
NO CLUE WHAT
LOVE WAS.

THIRTEEN

GREEN EYES

HAVING PAID penance to God and the church, I was permitted to resume my studies. I felt that I still had a calling on my life and I was determined to fulfill it.

One of the required courses for my degree was *Marriage and Family*. The classroom where the course was taught had three rows of desks in it. My seat was in the middle, toward the back of the room. Only days after classes began I noticed a gorgeous angel-shaped brunette in the row diagonally behind me. Her emerald eyes twinkled daringly with mischief. They would make a man stop cold in his tracks before approaching her. While she was hot and attractive, the way she moved, the way she spoke, the way she carried herself all conveyed, without saying a word, that this woman was to be taken seriously.

Although we started college the same year, I did not officially meet Elena until a year into our studies. We moved in different circles, and my mind was preoccupied with another.

In 1999, before all hell broke loose, I played a character in a Halloween production the church we attended put on. Elena was the costume designer. Our paths crossed for the first time then. Barely twenty, I was still acting like a teenager. The day I met her, acting a clown, I ran into a wall—on purpose—for God knows what reason and bounced off it. She looked at me, shaking her head in disbelief.

"Are you okay?" she asked, meaning more mentally than physically.

That year would prove that I was not.

It was not until the winter of 2001 that my eyes would settle on her face, my heart skipping a beat each time. I did not want this feeling. I was not welcoming it. I just had a taste of what relationships could turn into. But as a blade of grass is drawn toward the sun for its survival, I was drawn to her. I could not get her out of my head.

Day after day, I would sneak glances at her, afraid she would notice. Frequently, she would catch me staring. She was beautiful, proper, surrounded by a group of friends I was not yet ready to penetrate, and frankly, I was scared of her. She was not like any other woman I had met. Her posture conveyed that attention from me or anyone else of the male species would not be welcomed. My roommate and a few more men from our church were all pining after her, but she would not give them the time of day. She was focused on academics and pursuing her life's purpose. Nothing was going to deter her. So, I did the next best thing a man could do to wiggle his way into a woman's life—I became friends with her best friend.

Stephanie, my sister from another mister, a full-blooded Liberian, was my way in. To get close to Elena, I would have to charm Stephanie first. While other men fell by the wayside, failing in their efforts to command her attention, I was going to strike for her heart. The art of romance was in the making.

As I got closer to Stephanie, I had an excuse to start speaking to Elena, each time falling for her a little more. Was it her killer looks, her integrity, her no-nonsense personality, her wit, or her self-confidence oozing out of her every pore that drew me in? I don't know. But I was magnetically attracted to her with each encounter.

In the spring of 2001, we both graduated from college. It was then that the Universe unleashed its blessings on me, and made me realize that even my mess and expulsion were a part of a grand plan to bring redemption into my life.

Elena and I started our studies at the same time. While I was expelled from my misconduct, Elena was forced to take a break from school at the same time, for financial reasons—she did not have enough money to pay for the classes required to complete her degree. Had her financial situation been different, I would have never met her. But heaven's conspiracy on my behalf did not stop there.

For the three years prior, I took frequent walks at the local park called "Blacklick." This was my place to contemplate, to dream and meditate while keeping my body in motion. For the same three years, Elena did the same, but our paths had not crossed, as if the Universe itself was keeping her hidden from me until the perfect time.

On a fated day in June, a week after graduation, I went for my daily stroll. I was dressed in baggy jeans, a blue T-shirt with a yellow checkered cotton shirt over it. I had a New York Yankees cap pulled over my eyes and heavy Timberland boots on my feet. I looked like a disaster. As I stepped onto the path, I froze dead in my tracks.

There, heading toward me was Elena. Her curves prominently showed through her workout suit, impossible to ignore. Black pants and a shirt with green stripes on the sides. Short curly hair proudly gracing her scalp and a big smile on her face. The mischievous look in her emerald eyes had me lose my ability to speak. I stood still, unable to move.

"Hi, Demetrye!" she said, coming near me. "Fancy seeing you here. Is this your first time here?"

I said nothing, my eyes darting side to side. What do I do?

"I am just leaving, but would you like company?" she asked, her eyes piercing deep into mine as I tried to avert them.

I might have muttered something under my breath, but she did not hear it, because she said, "So, you are not going to invite me? If you prefer to be alone, I'll keep walking."

Finally, I forced my tongue to move.

"No! Please, do come," was all my mouth could formulate.

Twisting around on her foot, she faced in the direction from which she just came.

"Okay! Let's go."

I was not used to this. She was not a typical American woman. I could see why she intimidated me and her numerous admirers so easily. She was what she thought. There was no pretense about her. Youngest of fourteen, raised with seven brothers, she was not shy or awkward with the opposite sex. She was at ease with herself, and her conversation flowed easily, making me relax in my own skin.

That day was the beginning of my journey to freedom. I just did not know it yet. She was to be my saving grace. She just did not know it yet either.

After our first encounter, I frequented the park to ensure that we ran into each other, "accidentally" appearing when she was there. Our walks and our conversations became a drink of fresh water for me. I thirsted for them. I was beginning to fall for her.

I was not her first admirer, and with her K-9 senses, Elena had me figured out before our first walk. She did not seem to care, neither did she have any intentions to reciprocate my feelings. Where she came from, men and women had platonic relationships as a cultural norm. In my world, to be friends with a woman was to be in love or lust with a woman. However, I was tired of hanging out with my buddies since restricting female company after Tracy's accusations and longed to have a female friend without any physical attachments. These two worldviews caused tension and confusion in my mind. I was in for a crazy learning curve.

Less than two weeks later I knew I was kidding myself thinking we could just be friends. I was falling for her at the speed of light. It did not help that she was a great cook in addition to looking like a goddess. Her mashed potatoes served up with Russian burgers (kotlety) and tomato salad, which I tasted on my first visit to her apartment, made me want to slap my momma and tell my daddy to get out. I was hooked! I had to have this woman! She was smart, beautiful, cultured, spoke four languages, had a beautiful soul, and could throw it down (this means that she could cook like the best of them). Only a fool would let this treasure slip away.

So, two weeks later I told her that I liked her. In the American sort of way. "I like you," rather than "I think you are amazing and I am interested in you."

She told me that she liked me too ... as a friend. She told me that if we were to continue our friendship, I would have to keep my feelings at bay. It seemed there was no chance for reciprocation.

However, I am a man of impulses. While this would have deterred someone else, I was not ready to concede. Two weeks later I dropped the next bomb ... over the phone.

"I want to marry you, Elena," I said.

"You what?" She sounded shocked. A pause. "And, what kind of man would say this kind of thing over the phone?"

"Okay, wait," I responded.

Before she could say another word, I hung up the phone, jumped in my car, and was on my way to see her.

"Oh my god, oh my god, oh my god, oh my god, oh my god, oh my god, oh my god ... " was a singular thought spinning in my mind like a tornado. I would have been grateful for the ground to tear asunder and swallow me up. I would have no objections to an early death. But I was committed.

It was eleven at night. Not to disturb Stephanie, who was not only Elena's friend but also her roommate, Elena stepped outside when I knocked on the door. We made our way to a bench by the pond. The fountain was absorbing the sound of our conversation so no one could hear us.

"Okay, I'm listening," Elena said as we sat down. "What is it that you want to tell me?"

"I ... WANT TO ... MARRY ... YOU ... " I squeezed the air out of my lungs to form words, all the while feeling like I was having an out-of-body experience.

"You do? Hmmm.... Wouldn't you need to love the person you want to marry?" She drilled her gaze into my face.

"Of course," I responded, not knowing what else to say.

"Do you know what love is, Demetrye?" she asked, my heart melting at the sound of her voice while also skipping beats in terror of the unknown.

Like a D student hoping for his teacher to not call on him, I knew this was my moment of reckoning.

The love that I had experienced so far was always served up with a side of violence, humiliation, and betrayal. Perhaps it was not love at all. The love I had for Tracy, the woman who was to have my child, was like a shrub with shallow roots—it toppled over at the first sight of difficulty.

In truth, I had no clue what love was. But something deep inside longed for who Elena was. Was that love? Lust? Fatal attraction? I did not know. But I knew that I wanted to be with her.

"No. I do not," I finally admitted. "But I am willing to learn if you show me."

This is where, in the American romance movies, the girl falls for the boy and they live happily ever after, learning how to love each other. Not in my story. This story had a Russian twist.

"Demetrye, it is not my job to teach you love. And it is not my calling. I do not want to be your teacher. And I am not in love with you. If you need someone to love and marry, you have to look elsewhere."

Silence. My head was spinning from the rejection. I felt seasick.

"But I can be your friend," she added.

I didn't know how to respond or what to feel. She had just rejected and accepted me at the same time. No punishment. No reward. She was not turned off by my ineptitude in love, nor did she want to take advantage of my vulnerability. She respected me.

Rather than wanting to run away, I yearned to stay. I still wanted to be near this amazing creature. A long conversation ensued. Three hours later, we said our goodbyes.

As I drove home, rather than feeling hopeless, I felt like I was given a chance to prove myself.

"I will become her friend," I thought. "I will learn how to love, and I will still have her as mine."

I WAS SO USED
TO PAIN AND
DISAPPOINTMENT
THAT HER
GENEROSITY
TOOK ME BY
SURPRISE.

FOURTEEN

LEARNING TO LOVE

ELENA, A first-generation immigrant, was born and raised in the former Soviet Union. She was both book and street smart, multilingual, easygoing, a deep thinker with a no-time-to-waste attitude, an introvert who could become an extrovert on demand, and authentic to a fault.

Raised by very devout and devoted parents, showered with love and support, she knew no obstacle too big to overcome. In her world, everything was possible. If she wanted something, she was willing to put hard work in to get it.

She lived by a motto: "It's not a matter of IF, it's a matter of WHEN." Her world was the making of her imagination and hard work. She did not believe in waiting for miracles to happen. She created miracles herself. She was the polar opposite of who I was.

Early on Elena learned how to withstand the hardest trials in her life without caving to pressure. Raised by Christian parents in a Communist country, her path was chosen for her—persecuted for her faith by authorities since early childhood. She would not be scared by her peers or swayed by them. She marched to the beat of her own drum.

She learned how to make friends in a hostile world. Always the protector of those who were weaker, she was not afraid to stand up for herself or others. As early as first grade, she already commanded the respect and love of her classmates and teachers. Stellar in academics—a straight A student—she was also stellar in humanity.

"There are no strangers. We are all one," she would tell me as I began to open my heart to the art of her love. "We cannot judge another person's dysfunction without knowing their full story." She could find something great in even the most despicable people.

Elena was laser focused on what she wanted from life. Unlike me, she chose to exclude romantic entanglements from her life while in college. Not that she was not capable of loving. Rather, with her pragmatic mind, she figured that she did not have time to gamble her emotions on something that might or might not work out and could distract her from being present and joyful every moment. She had no room for heartbreak.

"Who has time for heartbreak?" she would say. "I am too busy living."

If she were ever to be with someone, she was committed to doing it only once. Like a swan.

It was this world that I entered in the summer of 2001. A world full of possibilities, focus, forgiveness, acceptance, and encouragement.

As days and months of our friendship passed, I felt my soul rest. I felt I could tell her everything about myself. Almost everything. I was still ashamed of the darkness in me.

Still succumbing to my sexual proclivities. I thought that if she were to learn about them, I would be banished from her life. My truth was too shameful to share with someone as pure as her. How could she not judge someone like me? Little did I know that she already knew more than she was supposed to.

Elena worked at the college we attended. She ran the Admissions Office, both domestic and international. She was lovingly called "Ms. Elena" by her adoring students. And Ms. Elena had access to every single file on campus ... including mine.

On one of our walks at the park, we sat down to chat. The conversation ebbed and flowed, until I said, "There is still so much about me that you don't know and I cannot share with you."

She was quiet for a moment, then finally responded softly, looking directly into my crumbling heart.

"But I already do."

A pause.

"Demetrye, I read your file months ago. You do not need to hide anything from me."

My heart dropped into my gut. She knew about my secret all along. I felt exposed and ashamed. I was judging myself. Yet, I could not see judgement in her eyes. It felt like my heart stopped beating. I could not breathe. There was not much I could or wanted to say. I only wanted to disappear.

So I did.

Ashamed, I stopped calling and seeing Elena for the next couple of weeks. I missed her company terribly, but did not dare take the first step.

Eventually, she tracked me down.

"What happened?" she asked as she sat next to me on the church pew.

I couldn't find it in myself to lie. She probably already knew anyway.

"Why would you want to be around someone like me?" I responded, as if I had leprosy.

Tilting her head slightly to the side, she squinted her eyes.

"So, you made this decision to end our friendship unilaterally? You did not want to bother to ask what I think?"

I had nothing to say.

"Friends don't do that, Demetrye. Friends have the decency to communicate before cutting one another out of their lives. So, why don't you figure out if we are friends, then ask what I think before making my decisions for me."

And she was gone. I felt torn more than ever before. I judged myself, yet she did not. I was so used to pain and disappointment that her generosity took me by surprise. She was a giver of second chances. She made me feel that my past and my struggles did not define me.

As I would get to know her more, I would learn that she believed anyone can change if they truly wanted to. There were no unchangeable or hopeless people in her world. There were only those who did or did not work toward their freedom. Those who wanted it and those who did not. She lived by Johann Wolfgang von Goethe's quote:

Treat a man as he is and he will remain as he is. Treat a man as he can and should be, and he will become as he can and should be.

Shame aside and truth be told, I was not ready to give up. I wanted her friendship. I wanted her in my life. I wanted to experience the true acceptance and forgiveness she offered, even if there was no chance for romance. So, I called her and apologized.

The more time I spent with her, the more I saw a world

of new possibilities. She treated me as the best version of myself. The person I did not yet know how to be. I could not help but begin to live up to those possibilities. Though never asking me to change, she was transforming my life. I couldn't help but to fall for her even more.

As our friendship grew, I began to learn what love is by observing Elena. She made love easy. No qualifiers, except to be the best version of myself. No alterations to my personality were necessary to be accepted by her. My wounds and my demons were welcome into her presence, although the demons were not welcome to stay. It would be up to me to chase them away.

If there was one thing Elena believed in, it was continual growth. Not the overnight kind of transformation that would leave you wondering who you truly are. But rather the steady and slow kind—improving by "one percent to infinity," as she would say. Every single day. Each day growing and improving on the day before.

I was learning. I was hopeful. I was in love and looking forward to each day.

Then 9/11 happened.

THE ONLY WAY TO HAVE HER—BODY AND SOUL— WOULD BE TO "PUT A RING ON IT" AND SIGN ON THE DOTTED LINE.

FIFTEEN

LOVE RETURNED

On September 11, 2001, Elena was flying to visit her family. When the news of the first plane crashing came, no one knew how many planes were hijacked or where. I spent the day pacing and praying that she was not on one of them. I could not lose her now that I had found her.

"Where are you?" I asked her when I finally got a hold of her. She was in Michigan. All planes were grounded, and she could not continue her trip to Washington.

"Tell me one word and I am there. I can drive up to get you," I offered.

Not needing to be rescued, "I got it," she responded. "I will rent a car and drive myself back."

I was left to pace my apartment in anticipation. In light of the circumstances, I realized how fragile life is. When she drove back to Ohio the day after, I decided to take a chance to tell her what she meant to me. Still "just friends," when I saw her, all I wanted to do was scoop her into my arms and never let go.

"I love you, Elena," I said the moment she got out of the car. "And yes, I know what love is."

It felt amazing to say it, and I was confident I had the seedling of the true knowledge of love sprouting in my heart.

She gave me a hug and reminded me that she was not looking for a romantic relationship. Friends—yes. Lovers and spouses—a hard pass.

Having survived my first rejection, I was in it for the long haul. I was not going to run away this time. Very soon I would have another chance to throw my hat into the ring for her heart.

A couple of months later, as the post 9/11 scare settled, Elena completed her trip to visit her family. When she returned, something had changed—my Russian Princess began to show signs of romantic interest in me. Slowly, her "we are just friends" grew to "love" as my heart did backflips and a happy dance.

On a cold December night in downtown Columbus, I professed my love for her one more time. She looked at me, measuring out her every word, as if to make sure I heard it the first time she said it.

"I love you too, Demetrye."

Surprised and blown away, I was excited.

I love her. She loves me. I felt like I finally knew what love was. My heart found peace after years of turmoil and heartbreak.

Our first kiss was magical. It was as if it was the first kiss of my life. Enrapturing, and intense as the Fourth of July fireworks.

By now I knew if Elena said "I love you" it was equal to "I love you and I will marry you, persistent fool." But I also knew to tread lightly. Unlike my relationship with Tracy, I knew that the only way to have her—body and soul—would be to "put a ring on it" and sign on the dotted line. I was more than happy to do both. There were no doubts!

I did not want to be apart from this woman ever again, come hell or high water. She was out of my league and I think she knew it. I would have been a fool to let her go. I was done with my past, ready to let go of my weaknesses. I felt like I hit the jackpot, but also still felt unworthy of her love. I would do whatever it took to prove myself and to hold onto her including a ring, a wedding, and a white picket fence.

And so, our courtship began, and our love, a tender bamboo shoot, was about to face harsh realities. Only time would show if it could survive.

SHE ALLOWED ME
TO GO THROUGH
MY DYSFUNCTION,
HOLDING MY
SECRETS, BEARING
MY PAIN.

SIXTEEN

MADE TO LAST

April 2002 took us both by surprise. It all started with me experiencing frequent headaches. One day, when I planned to take Elena on a date, my work partner and I were out delivering a furniture order. I had a migraine so intense that over-the-counter painkillers could not relieve it. Then suddenly, my eyesight was gone. Had I been behind the wheel that day, we both might have died. It took a few minutes before I could see again.

Instead of a date, Elena took me to the emergency room. After bloodwork, CT scans, and an MRI, I was diagnosed with a cyst in the right ventricle of my brain and was immediately admitted. The pressure from cerebrospinal fluid, which was rapidly building up in my skull, could have forced the brain down and caused paralysis or even death.

Three days later, in the hands of one of the most skilled brain surgeons in the U.S., I underwent a brain surgery.

Thankfully the cyst was benign and besides some short-term memory lapses, I was expected to have a full and speedy recovery. However, in a matter of days the prognosis of a quick recovery turned into a month-long stay at the hospital.

I developed an infection of the cerebrospinal fluid and my condition quickly deteriorated. I was in constant pain. Even a light touch would send me into a whirlwind of agony. The doctors, who told me that I would walk out of the hospital unscathed only days ago, now insisted on surgically inserting a shunt into my head. My body was storing too much cerebrospinal fluid inside the skull. Unless I wanted to risk death, I would need a shunt to dump extra fluid into my stomach cavity.

I had a choice to make. If I chose the procedure, I could never play contact sports again and my range of activities would be limited for life. Additionally, the shunt would have to be replaced every five to ten years. That meant more surgeries, more setbacks, and a possibility of additional complications.

The surgery had affected my short-term memory and my ability to process complicated situations. I was incapable of making a sound decision for myself, so all decision-making fell to Elena. I had signed the Power of Attorney to her. It was now up to her to decide what happened to me. My fate and my life were in her hands.

She surprised us all.

"Absolutely not!" she responded to the doctor's recommendation. "There will be no shunt unless it is the very last resort. We will be here as long as it takes for you to figure out how to fix this situation."

She was twenty-six and feisty as hell. I had been surrounded by strong women all my life, so her strength and resolve did not intimidate me. Rather, I embraced it. And by now I had nothing but trust and admiration for her. The doctors and the Universe would have to bend to her will.

For the next three weeks as my body was fighting off the infection, I fought for my sanity.

I was allergic to codeine, the painkiller I was prescribed. It was administered several times a day to manage post-surgery pain. While it provided much needed relief, I felt high, disconnected from reality, and lost in hallucinations.

In this drug-induced state, I spent my time chasing red smurfs while never getting out of bed. I saw the clock talk to me and had imaginary flings with my nurses. That world seemed real. You could not have convinced me otherwise.

As I recounted my escapades to Elena, she deduced that it was not my recovering brain playing tricks on me, but a reaction to the medication. She began to push for an alternative—morphine. The attending physician on my case refused to comply, insisting that morphine was highly addictive and I would have to do without it. It did not take long for the situation to come to a head.

One night I woke up disoriented. Sliding between reality and hallucinations, I felt my way around in the dark. My hand landed on my head. There was something stuck in it. I freaked out. I scraped and scratched at it furiously until I got it out. At last I was free of it! As I felt a sense of relief, the machines began to blare. Nurses flooded my room. It turned out that I pulled out the tube that was draining excess fluid from my skull!

Creating a makeshift O.R. in my room, the doctors performed the second surgery, drilling a new hole in my skull. Elena caught the end of it as she arrived for her early morning visit. She was done! Seeing me tied to my bed in restraints, sedated and helpless, her patience was pushed too far.

Pulling the attending aside, she said, "You either get him off this medication or I am going to make sure you no longer have your job."

This time he complied. My sanity was restored as soon as I was switched to morphine and I began to recover.

The doctors were still pushing for a shunt and Elena was still fighting for my right to stay at the hospital as long as needed for a complete recovery. She wanted me to walk out without a shunt and without limitations. Medical bills were already piling up, so what would a few more days at the hospital do? To her, it was not about the money. It was about the quality of life I would have after all was said and done.

During my month-long stay at the hospital, Elena worked a full-time job and spent every waking moment she could in my hospital room. Without her I was unable to relax or sleep. I was always aloof, my brain desperately trying to reconnect its disturbed neural connections and make sense of the world around me.

After my drug-induced incident I was placed in restraints so I would not make another attempt. Elena would not have it. She saw that being tied to the bed scared me and left me feeling helpless and demented. After another round of arguments with doctors, she got her way. I was out of restraints and placed under twenty-four hour supervision by hospital appointed sitters.

I felt safe out of restraints, and even safer because she was in my life. Not yet married, she already showed that she was in this for the long haul. She was not scared off by my emotional struggles, the physical limitations I was facing, or the looming medical debt.

I felt even more fortunate after overhearing how my next-door neighbor's fiancée fell apart and walked out on him. The guy was in a terrible car crash. His body maimed and burned, his future seemingly bleak. While his parents rallied around him, his fiancée could not take the pain and the unknown and walked out of his room and his life. I was a lucky man to have a woman who was not scared by my mess.

After all these years, I was still in touch with the Browns who stayed uninvolved during the surgery and the recovery process, except for the first week when they insisted that the hospital transport me to New Jersey for a second opinion. Since it made no medical or financial sense, I pushed back. Anne came out to see me right after the surgery but only for a day. Then it was back to my Russian Beauty and me.

Since Elena came from a very tight-knit family where everyone was involved in each other's lives, she felt obligated to keep the Browns abreast of all unfolding events regardless of how tired she was or how unappreciative they seemed. Not so much as a "thank you" from them, while Elena's siblings were lining up with offers to fly out to Ohio to support us.

With my brain off codeine and now having a morphine drip on demand, I was still in and out of reality, lost between a make-believe world and the tangible world around me. From hallucinating that I was locked in a room with a demon, to Elena duping me into thinking we were married with kids (she deserved to have some fun at my expense), everything seemed like a reality to me.

Once, I was convinced that George, the janitor, and I were out doing a delivery in a Rent-A-Center truck, a company I worked for before landing in the hospital. In my drug-induced imagination, George and I delivered a couch to a female client. She was so into me that she gave me her phone number. I had to tell Elena. Since I was bed-bound, she did not buy my story. However, I was so convinced that

I was right, that I insisted that she should check my pant pockets for the woman's number. Of course, there was no phone number or even pants in my room. Instead of arguing with my crazy, Elena went along with my make-believe reality, careful not to upset the delicate balance of my mind. Anything to keep me happy and non-argumentative.

While drugs make some people violent, morphine brought a flirt out in me. When I was not stealing imaginary hearts on furniture deliveries with George, I was charming my way into real hearts, particularly that of Danny, a shy nurse's assistant.

A woman of a few words, Danny came alive when we were alone. Before long, she was sneaking contraband from the hospital's kitchen for me—chocolate chip cookies. She found reasons to spend time chatting with me and was never happy when Elena came around. Danny had a crush on me. However, there was only one woman on my mind. The only one who still found me to be a prize, despite my pitiful condition—bed bound, tubes sticking out of my head, and in a dire need of a shower (a far cry from the GQ model I imagined myself to be when on morphine).

Since I could not get out of bed, sponge baths were my only option to stay clean. This meant that someone would have to see me helpless and naked. There was no way I was going to let that happen. No nurse would see me in my birthday suit! I would rather stink than feel humiliated.

However, a few days after the surgery, stubbornness aside, I knew I had to get freshened up. With much persuasion, I finally caved to let Elena wash me. Feeling helpless and embarrassed, I rolled over on my side, as she washed me from head to toe. Desperate to preserve some dignity, much to Elena's relief, I insisted on washing my manhood myself. Some things needed to stay a mystery.

I had come full circle with Elena. From feeling fully exposed with my struggles, to being naked and (almost) not ashamed. She had seen all there was to see of me, figuratively and physically. Yet, she didn't run.

Feeling helpless was not easy for me. I wanted to feel like "a man," able to take care of myself. And it was not easy for Elena to become my entire universe—working by day, taking care of me by night, often leaving the hospital after midnight, way past the visitation hours, only to start her morning at five the next day. Physically exhausted, yet she never complained. There was always a smile on her face the moment she stepped into my room, throwing the curtains open to welcome daylight. She would read healing affirmations to me, go through my finances, wash me, brush my hair, and even spoon-feed me at times. Since my ability to form complete sentences and my short-term memory were affected, she even learned to read my mind and finish my thoughts so my visitors and the hospital staff could make sense of my ramblings.

After the surgery, my memory was not the only thing affected. I became blunt in my speech. If it was on my mind, it was coming out of my mouth. After the surgery I had a lot of cravings. I craved everything from Wendy's chicken nuggets and fries to Cherry Coke, KFC, and cereal. Elena was at my beck and call. If I wanted something, she got it for me.

One morning I was craving Captain Crunch cereal. Thinking of Crunch Berries happily popping in a bowl of milk made my mouth water. Unable to steer the spoon into my mouth, my coordination still off, I was at Elena's mercy to satisfy my craving. She filled the spoon and aimed at my mouth, waiting for me to take a bite. Then the next one and the next. The spoon was on standby, filled with the next mouthwatering bite when I needed it. At some point, to my confused brain, things were going just a little too fast.

"Stop shoving it!" I said angrily, my voice rising.

"What?" She looked surprised.

"Stop shoving the food into my mouth. You're going too fast." I was losing my patience fast.

Stephanie, who had been cheerfully reclining in a chair chatting me up, averted her eyes.

"Stephanie, would you step out for a moment?" Elena asked.

Relieved at the permission to escape, Stephanie darted for the door. Then came my moment of reckoning.

"Listen," Elena measured each word patiently, "I get that this is not a picnic for you. I cannot even imagine how hard this is. You are the one feeling like you are losing your mind. So listen: I am here for you. I have been here and I am not going anywhere. But hear me and hear me clearly ... " she paused for the words to sink in. "This will be the first and the last time you ever disrespect me like this. Is that clear?"

Yes! It was definitely clear. This brain of mine would need to cooperate if I wanted to have a caring Russian Princess rather than an angry Russian Bear.

Lesson learned. Falling out of grace with Elena would be equal to suicide for me. She was not only my saving grace and in charge of making my health decisions, she was the extension of my brain and my mouthpiece. By now, she also knew my social security number and had all the dirt on me. If anyone could mess up my life and get away with it—it would be her. She was also my anchor, reassuring me with her presence and her unwavering certainty that I will get my full healing, despite the dim prognosis. I decided I better tread more lightly next time.

Elena became my sanity, my hope, my faith. She understood my dysfunction. She did not approve of it, but she did not judge me for it. And rather than giving up on me or shunning me, she allowed me to go through my dysfunction, holding my secrets, bearing my pain. She placed me in the safe zone of herself, as if she were a containment vessel where I could explode with my past and future failures without destroying others in my wake ... except for her.

Four weeks after the surgery, I left the Ohio State University Hospital just as we resolved I would—infection and shunt-free. This was a miracle beyond any miracles I ever witnessed. I had everything I wanted and was headed for full recovery.

However, I think the Universe wanted to give us another opportunity to grow in our faith. I was back two weeks later. The infection came back full force, ravaging my body. My skin was too sensitive to touch, my head splitting with vicious headaches. It seemed that the only way forward was to resign myself to the surgeon's recommendation and get the shunt. I did not know what else to do. Still not fully capable of making sense of things, I deferred to Elena again.

She was not willing to concede. Not yet.

At the hospital, once the labs and MRI results were in, she told the doctors to treat me as they did before, planning for a full recovery.

"We are not ready to throw in the towel," she told them. "Do what you need. We are expecting a miracle."

"Ma'am," responded the attending physician, "I respect your faith, but it is time to face the facts. Demetrye requires a shunt. His body is unable to deal with the excess cerebrospinal fluid on its own."

She was unyielding. If we did it once, we should be able to do it again. I was admitted for another two weeks. One more procedure. One more hole in my head to relieve the pressure. We were back to our daily practice of affirmations, prayer, and visualizations, expecting nothing short of a miracle.

Elena was militant about everything that surrounded me day and night. She knew that I needed to believe as much as she did for the impossible to happen. So much so that she would not allow anyone in my hospital room who did not believe that I could be fully healed. Crazy, but it worked!

Two weeks later I walked out of the hospital a free man for the second time, returning only for annual checkups. Four years in a row, we came back. Each year, my neurosurgeon was surprised at my progress.

"Based on your scans," he told me on my two-year anniversary, "if I were not your surgeon and there was no scar on your head, I would have never known there was anything wrong with you. Your brain looks good as new."

After getting out of the hospital, I spent the next three months living with Elena and Stephanie, taking over their living room. I could not yet function on my own or return to work—my full brain's capacity would take over two years to restore, and I needed someone to ensure my safety and wellbeing.

After two infections I was prescribed a lengthy round of antibiotics and steroids. These medications had to be administered intravenously via a PICC line several times a day. Since I was not yet allowed to drive because I would be a danger to myself and anyone on the road I had only two options: have a nurse visit me three times a day, which meant further financial burden, or have someone I could trust do it for me. Naturally, Elena took it upon herself to help. I had no one else I would trust with my life.

She got trained to administer medication on a very strict schedule. Once in the morning, before heading off to work. Once at lunch time, which meant she did not get to have real lunch breaks for nearly three months. And once in the evening. While feeling helpless was not what a grown man would want, I was grateful to have her in my corner. Elena, Stephanie, and their circle of friends became my family.

As I recovered, my brain looked for consistencies, similarities, and repetition. I had attempted to read books but found myself rereading the same several pages over and over, never retaining any of it.

There was a movie, however, that gave me the sense of sanity I was looking for—*One Fine Day*, with George Clooney and Michelle Pfeifer. It's a movie about an overworked single mother who falls in love with a sarcastic single father after a torturous day of losing and finding their children. So while the girls were out at work, I binge watched this movie. There was something about it that gave my brain a sense of safety and stability. Some days I watched it four or five times in a row. Every time I watched it was as if it was the first time.

Every night when the girls got home, I begged them to watch it with me. For their healthy brains, after the first couple of weeks, it became torture. They looked for ways to escape the *One Fine Day* purgatory. After about a month of watching and rewinding the tape repeatedly, the VCR broke with the tape in it. Elena and Stephanie sent up a prayer of gratitude as I mourned my loss. However, while the VCR was done for, I managed to rescue the tape and have it to this day.

I never had a lazy bone in my body. If anything, while living with the Browns I learned to pull my weight. So when not watching *One Fine Day* or attempting to make progress on the same few pages of a book, I stayed busy cleaning. I did it to pull my weight and to demonstrate my gratitude for all the girls did for me. By the time Elena and Stephanie got home, the house was always spotless.

NO ONE TOUCHES
A BLACK MAN'S
HAIR EXCEPT FOR
HIS BARBER.

SEVENTEEN

BLACK MAN'S HAIR

WHILE WELL versed in cross-cultural communications, Elena had a lot to learn about the quirks of a Black man.

There was a two-inch-long hole in my skull, barely covered with skin and two smaller ones to accompany it. It would take years for the skull bone to grow back. In the meantime, you could see cerebrospinal fluid pulsating under the skin on my head, as you would with an infant's fontanelle. Since the surgeons had to shave my skull where they drilled, my hair looked like a neglected landscape.

If you know anything about Black men, you know that we are obsessively particular about our hair. After the surgery, Elena got schooled on just how far my hair obsession went.

Normally, I got my hair cut twice a month. Not just any barber would do. I found mine in the north part of Columbus, nearly forty minutes away from where I lived, and religiously went only to him. Like any good Black barber,

Ike did not take appointments. First come, first served was his policy. This meant that if you did not get to his shop on time, you could spend hours waiting in line, which could be a religious experience in itself.

Barber shops are where Black communities come together. A home away from home, where we can talk unapologetically about anything—religion, politics, women, relationships, food—no topic is off the table. We can hang out and talk for hours, even after the hair is cut.

My haircut days had a flow to them. Up at four in the morning, grab breakfast to have my car parked by Ike's shop by five-thirty. Take a nap and be the first in line when Ike unlocked the doors at six.

Each hair was meticulously cut so I could achieve my perfect 360-degree wave look. I would brush each portion of my hair fifty times, so each hair would line up in the same direction. Then put on pomade and a wave cap. When everything was said and done, I was a vision to behold. I had "the good hair" and took pride in it.

Knowing this, imagine how horrified I was when Elena offered to give me a haircut to even out my after-surgery lopsided mohawk.

"You want to do what? Oh, no, babe! No one touches a Black man's hair except for his barber," I protested.

It took her a beat to come around but she got it. Dialing Ike, she put me on the phone to make an introduction, then explained my delicate situation to him. She wanted to be sure he was up to the task—not every barber would risk cutting hair on a sutured head.

The day of the haircut finally came. Elena packed me into the car, leaving early enough to beat the traffic. She had to drive slowly—my brain could not cope with being transported at higher speeds yet. Driving faster than thirty miles per hour overwhelmed me, inducing cold sweats and heart palpitations. She got me to Ike's shop in one piece. We parked the car and I took Elena into my world.

The moment we opened the door everyone fell silent. It was as if someone put life on pause. Barbers stopped cutting and sweeping the floor, patrons stopped speaking, even a fly froze in mid-air. What was a White woman doing in a Black barber shop?

Ike finally broke the awkward silence.

"What's up, Dee? Come here, have a seat."

And life resumed. Barbers went back to cutting, patrons to chatting, mothers to scolding their kids, and flies to flying. It felt like being back home.

Elena still got a few awkward glances, but she didn't care. She never did. Not with my family, not with friends or strangers, not with African American sisters complaining that she took one of their good ones. People could accept her or not, but she never cared about what people thought of her.

Elena never offered to cut my hair again. Not even a singular strayed piece. She understood the relationship Black men have with their hair. It is as sacred as marital bonds for many. Instead, she drove me to get my haircut by my barber until the day I could drive myself again.

MY NATIONALITY,
MY RACE, MY
UPBRINGING—
NONE OF IT
MATTERED.

EIGHTEEN

MEET THE RUSSIANS

IN THE fall of 2002, while still recovering, it was time to meet Elena's family. We'd been officially dating for over eight months and if I were to ever pop the question, I knew I had to meet the family first. I was nervous and scared.

The youngest brother of the family, Vlad, had visited Elena while I stayed with her post-surgery. Impressively built at six-foot-two, he looked like Ivan Drago from *Rocky IV*. Taking me outside while working on Elena's car, he glanced at me.

"That's my sister," he said nodding toward the apartment, his green eyes burrowing into mine, his words meaning more than he uttered.

"I got it. You have to say nothing else," I responded, holding his gaze as long as I could.

If he was any indication of what I had to go through on my visit, I braced myself in anticipation. She had six more brothers and six sisters for me to impress. Then there were the parents.

To prepare me, Elena took me to see *My Big Fat Greek Wedding*—a movie released in 2002 that painted a great cultural contrast between the American and the Greek cultures. The American family was reserved and individualistic. The Greek—loud, in-your-face and in-your-business, family and community oriented, loving and kind. While not Greek, Elena assured me that her family was equally loving and loud. She was not wrong.

On our arrival, we were picked up by one of the sisters and a nephew. If my hair ritual was a culture shock to Elena, the way Russians meet and treat their guests was mine. They arrived in style, with a bouquet of flowers in hand. After hugs, kisses, and laughter, we piled into the car. They wanted to know everything about me. EVERYTHING.

When we got to the house, I met the parents, Momma and Papa, the matriarch and patriarch of the clan, which numbered over one hundred immediate family members. Well prepared by Elena, I pulled out a gift for each. (Russians bring gifts for the hosts when they visit. Never visit empty-handed even if you are only coming to dinner.)

Exhausted by the trip I took a nap. It was not long before I was awakened by noise and commotion.

"Where is he? Where is he?" I heard voices of all ages coming from upstairs.

I dragged myself out of bed. Coming up to the second floor, I was nearly knocked off my feet. Like a stampede, they came at me—hugging, laughing, slapping my back, saying my name the way it is supposed to be said—DemetR-RRRye—rolling the 'R' as only Russians can.

In the days to follow we visited each of Elena's siblings. At every house, without fail, we were promptly invited to a table splitting at the seams with the best of their cooking. I did not know it was possible, but I was tired of eating. I did not know how to pace myself. I needed to leave enough room in my stomach for at least a small snack at each house, to be respectful toward our hosts. In a few short days of visiting the family, I got a crash course in Russian hospitality.

I quickly became "Uncle Demetrye" to Elena's nephews and nieces, who ranged from newborn to my age. In fact, at least four of them were older than me. Since I was with their aunt, however, I was to become their uncle.

I already had no doubt in my heart that I wanted to be with Elena. Now, having visited her family, the deal was sealed. I wanted to be a part of this crazy, loud, loving clan. It seemed these people did not have any inkling of what dysfunction like the one I grew up in meant. They were willing to sacrifice and die for each other. I wanted to learn how to love like them.

Most importantly, they accepted and approved of me. My nationality, my race, my upbringing—none of it mattered. I was a person they liked and grew to love, a man that their sister and aunt chose was the only factor that mattered. They immediately made me one of their own.

While not yet engaged, they knew Elena enough to know that if she brought me to meet the family, she was serious. To them, we were as good as engaged. The rest was just a formality.

SHE GOT ME, MY MESS, MY STRUGGLES, DESTROYED CREDIT, AND A HUNDRED THOUSAND DOLLARS IN MEDICAL BILLS.

NINETEEN

PUT A RING ON IT

THIRD TIME'S the charm.

Back in Columbus, the day finally came. I was ready to ask Elena to marry me again. Something was telling me she might say "Yes!" this time.

With her shrewd financial skills, over the six months of my recovery she helped me accumulate a nice cushion. No longer a broke student, I could buy my woman a ring. One that she deserved.

January 12, 2003, on a cold winter day, I was ready to propose. On the way to the jewelry store to pick up her ring, we got into a disagreement. I do not remember what it was about, but it was something that made both of us very upset. So much so that Elena stayed in the car while I picked up the ring. Not thinking it through, I still popped the question. This was not an over the top proposal. No name written in the sky, rose petals on the ground, photographer hiding in the bushes, or ring in a champagne glass. No forethought. No planning. Not even an apology for the argument. I went for it.

"So, will you marry me?" I asked her in the car, pulling out the ring box and placing it in front of her.

"Absolutely not!" she responded.

Maybe I should have waited for her wrath to wear off. But being romantic was not my strong suit. So I backtracked. And after a few minutes of proper apology, she put the ring on her finger. I was beyond myself, filled with happiness and pride.

She said YES!

It was time to plan the wedding.

Elena did not want anything big or extravagant. We were only one year post my brain surgeries. She was still emotionally exhausted from having to take care of me, and we had a mountain of medical debt. Elena's family offered to pay for the wedding and to fly us to Washington to have it there. It was tempting, but concerned that if we accepted we might offend the Browns, we declined. It was too far for them to drive from Jersey to Washington and my Black family did not believe in flying. If they decided to attend, they would have to travel by a bus or car. And I knew that they would not be willing to take such a long trip. So, rather than taking a chance at offending someone, we decided to keep it simple. Just the two of us along with a couple of witnesses was all we needed to be happy.

April 12, 2003, on the one-year anniversary of my brain surgery, we said our "I Do's" in a small private ceremony. Just us two, an officiant and his wife, two witnesses, and a couple of friends. We were husband and wife.

I got Elena. And she got me, my mess, my struggles, destroyed credit, and a hundred thousand dollars in medical bills.

There was nothing traditional about our love or our wedding. From our decision to elope to our vows, everything was designed by us and for us. Our vows were our stories, our way to express our love and commitment. We only said the words that needed to be said. Nothing more, nothing less.

Elena spoke her vows first:

Demetrye, when I least expected it, heaven sent you my way. From the moment I ran into you at the park, from our first walk together, I knew that you were a man of purpose. It was your ambition and your hunger for truth that drew me to you. I watched you overcome life's challenges and not let them bring you down. I observed you in your strengths and your weaknesses. Through it all, I saw a person I could depend on and believe in. I chose to love you for who you are and for who you want to be. I love you with every fiber of my being.

You became my best friend and my confidant. You are my first and only love. I am honored to have become your friend and, today, your wife. I treasure you. I will celebrate the joys of life with you. I promise to support your dreams and walk beside you, offering courage and strength when you need it.

I will listen to you when you speak, encourage you in times of doubt, comfort you in times of sorrow, and be a refuge of strength in times of uncertainty. I will be the wind beneath your wings and a shoulder you can cry on.

I will be faithful to you all of my days. I will be honest with you always. I will cherish, love, and respect you every moment of my life.

It was hard to follow that, but I had vows of my own:

This is my vow and covenant to you—to love, honor, and cherish you. To be there when times are rough and shaky. To esteem you as my better half. To be faithful, true, and pure before you. To be your shelter, your husband, best friend, and a forever companion. To be the love of your life, your never-ending fountain of desire and love.

Only one of us will live to keep the promises made that day.

PART FOUR

MISSING PIECES

I WAS HAPPY THAT
THE WINDS OF
TESSIE'S INSANITY
BLEW ME AS
FAR FROM THE
WILKINS TREE AS
POSSIBLE.

TWENTY
===

FAR FROM THE TREE

When Tessie passed and through the turbulent years that followed, I took on the Brown family as my own. Up until this point, they were the only family I needed. However, as I got to know Elena and her family, it was no longer enough. A part of me wanted to find my biological roots. I wanted to know the truth. Who was I? Who do I look like? Did my family love me? Did they want me? Did they ever look for me after Tessie's funeral? Time had buried the few memories I had of them. I wanted a sense of belonging and needed answers.

By this point I had only patchy memories of Tessie and almost none of Edward. There were too many holes in my remembering and no way to patch them up. Elena was determined to change that.

"If we are to have a family, I need to know where you come from," she told me, "so our children know their roots.

And I need you to have all your questions answered, so you have a sense of wholeness."

In 2002, when the movie *Antwone Fisher* came out, it became the push I needed to agree with Elena. It would be the beginning of my quest to find the family I never knew.

The movie was about an African American sailor who is prone to violent outbursts and is sent to a naval psychiatrist for help. At first, he refuses to open up, but eventually breaks down and reveals a horrific childhood of neglect and abuse—much like my own. Through the guidance of his doctor, he confronts his painful past and begins a quest to find the family he never knew, including finding and confronting his drug-addicted mother.

In so many ways, his story was like mine. I broke down watching it at the movie theatre. Tears and snot flowed freely as Elena grabbed my hand.

"We will find your biological family, Demetrye. I promise you," she committed, looking into my eyes.

At first, I felt a little apprehensive about finding them. The Browns painted them in an unfavorable light and I myself questioned their loyalty. None of them had ever come looking for me. But, putting apprehension and fears aside, I said yes to the endeavor. We committed ourselves to finding breadcrumbs that would lead us to them and bring me wholeness.

I reached out to the Browns. They certainly would know something about my biological family, I thought. But they denied me any information. Every question I asked was met by, "We don't know."

"Where was my mother buried?"

"We don't know."

"Where can I find either side of my biological family?"

"We don't know."

They and I knew that it was not true. They could not have had selective amnesia less than fifteen years after Tessie's burial.

My temper flared. I wanted to cut them off. If they could not meet me halfway, I owed them nothing. If they could not tell me the truth, I did not want them in my life. Had it not been for Elena, who believed that family is the biggest treasure we have, I would have severed my relationship with them for good without a second thought.

However, the desire to find my family did not stop me from living. Now newlywed, the time came for Elena and me to set out on our first big adventure. Right after getting married we relocated to Florida with the few belongings we had packed in a U-Haul. The eleven-year-old Demetrye who fell in love with Disney World and found his ability to dream in that magic place wanted to live out his fantasy.

We settled in the small town of Leesburg where Elena had a job offer. When we drove in, it felt like we time traveled to the 1960s. There was a slow pace of life, not many conveniences, segregation and racism still alive, although no one would admit it. Confederate flags at every turn. Locals calling outsiders "Yankees." Southern pride bumper stickers, one of which read: "NAACP is an acronym for: niggers, apes, alligators, coons and possums." The two of us stuck out like a sore thumb.

As we settled in and unpacked, we resumed the search for my family. With the little that we had, Elena traced my biological father to the point of his arrest, when he kidnapped Kat and me in 1983. We were able to get the public record of his release date. June 6th, 1987. And then his trail grew cold. No one knew where to find him.

Not giving up, we ordered a copy of my birth certificate from the Chatham County courthouse in Savannah, Georgia—my birthplace. Elena continued the search with the little information we could glean from it. She should have become a PI! She deduced that there was a possibility that my father's family had not migrated like Browns did. So using online resources, we pulled up every Wilkins family in Savannah and began cold calling them.

Thirty plus calls in, I had memorized the script we prepared. The responses I got were as unpredictable as humanity. Some were nice and wished me luck in finding my father. Others cursed me out and hung up. Yet others made threats they certainly could not fulfill.

Eventually I spoke with a woman who rather than answering my questions put me through a mini interrogation. Nearing a point of frustration, I asked her why she wanted to know so much about me since it was clear she was not a Wilkins.

"I know some Wilkinses, baby," she responded with a Southern drawl. "Give me a few minutes and I will get back to you. Okay, baby?"

An hour later my phone rang.

"This is Demetrye," I said.

"Yes, sweetheart, can you tell me your full name and what it is you are looking for?" came the sweetest elderly voice through the receiver.

"Yes. My name is Demetrye Wilkins, and I am looking for Edward Charles Wilkins who was born February 4, 1954."

"Do you mean February 5th, baby?" she asked.

"Yes," my heart skipped a beat. I held my breath in anticipation of what might come next.

"Well, if that's the case, I am his mother, Pearl Wilkins. I am your grandmother, baby."

The floor swirled under me. I sat on our bed to steady myself. Covering the receiver with my hand, I screamed,

"Elena, I found them! I found my grandmother!"

The emotion I felt was indescribable. It could rival the excitement I had over the first real Christmas at the Browns'. Excitement mixed with pure joy and a sense of completeness.

I stayed on the phone with Grandma Pearl for hours that day and every day after for the next couple of weeks until I could get time off work to meet her and the rest of the Wilkins family face to face.

As soon as my job would allow, Elena and I packed into our grey Honda Accord and headed to Savannah—a mere four-and-a-half-hour drive from where we lived.

I was filled with excitement. Truth be told, I felt a little nervous too. The closer we got to Savannah, the more the butterflies in my stomach were threatening to become a tornado, claiming the contents of my stomach. How are they going to react? Will they accept me? What do I say? What do I ask? Elena kept me from spiraling out with my ever-wandering mind.

Grandma's house was hard to miss. Freshly painted white siding with blue shutters and a blue roof to match, it had "WILKINS" spelled out right under the house number. Impatiently, with flowers in my hand, I rang the doorbell. Grandma Pearl stepped out, her eyes filled with tears, beaming ear to ear, her mouth missing dentures.

"Welcome home, baby." She squeezed me tightly in her motherly embrace.

I pulled back and soaked in every feature of her face. I was struck. I looked like her! There was no question in my mind that we were related. No DNA test required. She was my blood.

It was February 16, 2004, and life had given me a present. Elena was right—finding my family brought healing in a way that I did not expect. It filled the gaping hole in my heart that nothing else could ever fill. I finally knew that I had a beginning. I had roots. I belonged. The questions that repeatedly swirled through my mind for the last fifteen years about my biological family were now getting answered.

Over the next few hours, I met my cousins, aunts, and uncles. I had a family reunion to rival the one I saw in the *Antwone Fisher* movie. Looking through family albums, talking to them, and taking a tour around Grandma's small southern home where I spent some of my early days, memories came flooding.

I did not think I could possibly remember anything, since Tessie took us away from there when I was barely two. Yet, there they were, rushing back as if a secret compartment was unlocked in my still recovering brain. I ran my memories by Grandma, aunts, and uncles. Surprised, they confirmed the best and the worst of them.

Later that day, Grandma had a surprise for me. She pulled me into her small kitchen and asked me to grab two little bowls off the highest shelf. I could not believe my eyes. These were mine and Kat's cereal bowls. Grandma, grinning a toothless smile, told me that she kept them all these years, hoping that one day she would see us again.

My heart was overflowing with joy. I felt like the cracks of my tattered heart were getting patched up and pulled together. I drank in each moment.

Only one question remained—where is Edward? I'd had two weeks of phone calls with Grandma and other family members and no one told me where he was. Any time I inquired of his whereabouts, the conversation got redirected. Finally, seeing them face to face, I had to know.

"Grandma, where is Dad?"

It felt awkward to call him that. Edward was never a father to me. I called him "the sperm donor" most of my life. Yet for some odd reason, whether due to a desire to experience what it felt like to say "Dad" or not to hurt Grandma's feelings, I called him the three-letter word I never thought I would say in my life.

A deep sigh bubbled up from her chest.

"He's in jail, baby," she finally admitted, looking away.

"For what, Grandma?" I pressed.

She averted her eyes, too scared to tell the truth.

"It's a mix-up, baby. I know he is innocent," she responded hurriedly, wanting to bring the topic to a close. Her maternal heart refused to believe that her eldest could do anything wrong.

As I would find out later, Edward was in jail for aggravated assault against a woman. But for now, guilty or not, I had to see him. I wanted to know what my father looked like. Did I have any of his traits? Did I look like him? Why did he abandon us? Why did he never come looking for us after the kidnapping? I had questions. A lot of them. And he was the only person who could possibly answer them all.

After visiting with Grandma, my head and heart buzzing from the emotions of this bittersweet reunion, Elena, one of my aunts, and I piled into our car and headed to the Chatham County jail.

Having handed over our IDs to security, we were moments away from meeting Edward. As we headed down the long hallway, we heard heavy metal doors slam behind us, separating us from the world outside. As each step echoed against the jail walls, I could hear my heart beat louder, my brain suspended between reality and dream. I was about to live out my wildest desire. One that I didn't even know I could have until Elena entered my life.

We were escorted to the visitation room. Settling into hard chairs with a bulletproof glass separating us from an empty chair, we waited. Minutes later we heard, "Wilkins, window 5."

Elena squeezed my hand, "Are you ready, sweetheart? This is what you wanted."

"Yes, I am," was all I could say.

I waited. The moment was here.

A slender man shuffled in and sat in front of me. He had salt-and-pepper hair, big cow-size eyes, and his bottom lip was slanted to the side after a recent stroke. Edward Charles Wilkins sat in front of me.

"Hi ... Dad," I said and hesitated to say anything else.

He looked at me. "Hi, son."

Time froze while we studied each other's features.

"You look like her," he finally broke the silence. "You look like your mother."

Then quiet for another moment.

"What's your last name, son?"

An odd question to be asked by a man who nearly killed me.

"Wilkins," I responded.

A huge smile swept over his crying face. He was proud. Proud as if he had done something to earn the right for his name to live on through me.

"Dad?" It was still odd to say this sacred word, but in the moment I simply did not know what else to call him. "What happened? What happened between you and Mom? And why didn't you come looking for us?"

In the next fifteen minutes we spent together I learned his side of the story. Once we caught up to the kidnapping part, he spoke unapologetically.

"I was arrested when I brought you to Savannah. When

I got out, I told myself, 'I won't go looking for them. When they grow up, they will find me.' See, I was right! You ... YOU found me. You came looking. I told everyone and they would not believe me, but here you are."

He was beaming with pride, as if he had won the lottery. I could feel my wife, whose family would allow neither hell nor heaven to keep them apart from their children, bubble up with indignation. She was too proper to show it or to interrupt the little time we had together, but I knew that neither she nor I thought that this was a celebration-worthy moment.

Then Edward dropped a bomb. It came out of nowhere, blindsiding me.

"Your brother is here also," he said.

"My who? What?"

"Your oldest brother," he repeated, as if I was supposed to know this well-kept secret. I knew that Tessie had a child before shacking up with Edward. I remember meeting her. But a brother? I was floored.

Edward Charles Wilkins Jr., five years my senior, was Edward's firstborn and my half-brother. And he was in jail. The same jail as his father. My brain struggled to process it all.

"What is he in for? What did he do?"

"Rape and murder."

What?! It felt like a nuclear size explosion went off in the building. I had found my father. He was accused of rape. I had a brother. He was accused of rape and murder. And ... I share my name with them. I felt utter shame to be part of this family, along with anger that this sort of violence was so prolific in both my biological and adopted families.

As I regained my ability to breathe, I said a silent prayer, thanking God for yanking me out of the grip of this family.

Hellish or not, the life with the Browns seemed like a land of milk and honey compared to what my life could have been.

The meeting was over. I was silent. Elena gave me space to process my emotions.

As we walked back down the same corridor that led me to Edward, my heart was no longer racing. Rather, I could not feel it beat at all. In slow motion, one foot in front of the other, we made it to the entrance where my aunt waited for us. I had to jolt myself back out of this dream state. I could process it all later, but now, it was time to get out into the fresh air and meet more family. Truthfully, after the encounter I just had, I was questioning if I wanted to. What other shocking secrets would be uncovered?

In the years to come, I would learn that my sperm donor was a serial rapist. The first time he was incarcerated was the time he kidnapped Kat and me. There were at least four more cases after that. To this day I cannot understand why he was ever released, rather than living out his days in the only place he deserved to call his home—prison.

And my brother, whom I got a chance to meet the day after meeting Edward also while separated by bulletproof glass, was convicted of three murders and a rape that was meant to end in a murder, but the last victim survived. In 2007, Edward Charles Jr. was convicted of the horrific crimes he committed and sentenced. Three consecutive life sentences without a chance for parole.

These people were my blood. For a while, after meeting them, a part of me was disgusted to share their DNA. I wondered, if I had been raised by these wolves, would I have turned out just like them? They say that the apple doesn't fall far from the tree. Having met them, I was happy that the winds of Tessie's insanity blew me and Kat as far from the Wilkins tree as possible.

I stayed in Savannah for a few more days before heading home. With my questions answered, I had one more thing to accomplish before my tattered heart would feel completely whole—I had to find Tessie's side of the family. I hoped against all odds, that they might be different than the Wilkinses.

MY CHEST
CONVULSED WITH
SOBS AS I FINALLY
ALLOWED MYSELF
TO FEEL.

TWENTY-ONE

MORE THAN A WHORE

I MUST have tapped into something supernatural. It seemed like heaven was smiling on me, granting my every wish. Only a couple of days after we got home, I received a call from a number I did not recognize.

"Hello?" A soft southern female voice came through the receiver. "Is Demetrye there?"

"This is Demetrye."

"Demetrye, this is Etoy, your sister," she said, her voice trembling with tears.

The last piece of my life's puzzle was falling into its resting place. I found my sister! Only days after my visit, Etoy, who also lived in Savannah, ran into Grandma Wilkins, who told her about our reunion and gave her my number.

The last time I saw Etoy, which was only the second time I had ever seen her, was at Tessie's funeral. Back then, still a child, I avoided her. Now, all I wanted to do was to meet her, get to know her, hold her in my arms, and if she was the sister I hoped she would be, never let her go.

We hit it off immediately, as if we had always known each other. We spent hours catching up on life that we did not get to share.

Etoy provided me a list of phone numbers for my aunts and uncle—Tessie's siblings. In weeks to follow, I spent countless hours talking to them and Etoy.

Back in those days, there were no unlimited calling plans on cell phones and my phone bill was running high. But neither Elena nor I minded. What I had could not be measured by dollars and cents.

I don't know if it is possible to have too much joy. If it is, I was guilty of that pleasure. The stars aligned to answer my every prayer.

Two weeks later we were back on the road. This time heading to Yemassee, South Carolina, the birthplace of my mother and her entire family.

Five hours later we were there. We pulled into a gas station only minutes away from my aunt's house to freshen up. In a hurry, I locked the keys in the car. Aunt Cynthia, mom's sister, drove to pick us up.

The moment she stepped out of the car, wearing a bathrobe, slippers, and rollers in her hair, there was no question in my mind that we were related. I looked more like her than Tessie.

Lula Mae was still alive, looking much the same as I could remember her from Tessie's funeral, only with more gray hair and a few more wrinkles. I was overjoyed to see her. Her speech was still unclear, so I spent my time buttering her up with hugs and occasional kisses on the cheek.

Before long, aunts, uncle, and cousins began to pile in. Aunt Helen, Lula Mae's eldest, the family historian, hurriedly entered the room. Eyes filled with tears as she nearly snapped my neck in two with her tight embrace. All the love Tessie did not know how to give came rushing into my being through this motherly embrace.

"We looked for you for so long," she said, beating me to my question with her greeting. "We always prayed for a day to reunite with you. Each holiday we all wondered what it would be like to have you and Kat with us. And here you are."

She was still holding me tight in her arms, studying my every feature, too afraid to let go, as if I were an apparition.

Hours flew by as we caught up on more than fifteen years of separation. They wanted to know everything about me and about Kat. Even though I had not seen Kat in person since I was still in high school, I shared how we reconnected right around the time I met Elena and how we stayed connected over the years. I gave them Kat's phone number, so they all could get in touch with her as well.

As we were getting ready to sit down for a meal at Aunt Helen's house, I heard a sweet, familiar voice.

"Where's my brother at?"

It was Etoy! My long lost and now much-loved sister. I rushed toward her. Our bodies collided as she jumped on me, wrapping her legs around my torso. As I tightly held Etoy's petite coke-bottle-shaped body in my arms, we both melted into a waterfall of tears. Together at last. Kept apart by our mother's choice, separated by the Browns' decision to keep me in the dark about her whereabouts, there was nothing that would ever tear us apart again.

When we finely peeled away from each other, we stood, inches apart, staring at each other, memorizing every line and eyelash just in case this was a dream. It seemed like an eternity passed before I snapped back into reality. There was still more family to meet. Etoy had brought her four beautiful children with her—two girls and two boys, my nieces and nephews.

I had a family who shared my DNA and seemed normal! I felt like my weary soul had finally found its resting place.

Like in any good movie (and this certainly seemed like a movie), my aunts prepared a table overflowing with Southern delicacies—collard greens, corn bread, and oxtails. While I declined the latter, my very diplomatic Russian bride could not bring herself to offend the hosts. She politely forced them down, trying not to chew. This would be her first and only endeavor into Southern Black folk food.

The hospitality of my family was only surpassed by their love abundantly streaming directly into my heart. Older cousins were there, driving in from each direction their lives took them to welcome back their long lost relative. I got to know each one, asking a million questions, and sharing with them the few memories my brain kept of our times together during my childhood.

When the time was right, I asked my aunts to tell me as much as they could about their sister, my mother. There were still too many unsolved mysteries.

The truth that came out was hard and painful to absorb. However, I was no longer a child and could finally grieve Tessie as my mother and as a human being.

Shortly after getting married, Tessie found out that Michael Owens, her knight in shining armor, was not a knight after all. The bus driver, though more stable than most men she gave her body to, had a temper. It flared frequently, leading to physical abuse. I do not know if the pregnancy that ended in stillbirth ever gave her a break from violence, but things got worse the longer she stayed. On one occasion Etoy saw Michael hold a gun to Tessie's head.

After burying the only child she wanted, Tessie felt that

there was nothing left to live for. Her weary soul, having spent years chasing after love, while she had given up the only two tiny hearts who loved her unconditionally, reached a breaking point. She knew that she was chasing ghosts. Finally, she awakened to reality. Her heart, breaking from the loss of her newborn and the loss of all her hopes, wanted one more chance. This time she was going to look for love where it could be found—with her children.

Tessie reached out to the Browns.

"I want my children back, Liza," she pleaded. "They're all I have."

To protect us from the life they once rescued us from, Aunt Liza refused, but not in the most diplomatic manner.

"If you want your kids back, Tessie," she responded, "you can have them. But only if you pay us back for all the time we invested into them and the money we spent on their food, their clothes, shelter, and education."

Liza was well aware that this was one challenge Tessie could never rise up to overcome. She simply did not have what it took to fight for us.

Heartbroken and depressed, Tessie bought a one-way bus ticket from Jersey to Yemassee, never to be seen alive again by the Browns, Kat, or me. For the first time in her life, she ran to the people who had the capacity to love her, only this time it was too late.

By the time she arrived at Yemassee, she was barely recognizable. Thin and frail, she had become a ghost of her vivacious self. Tessie came home to die.

"I have nothing to live for, Helen," she told my aunt as she unpacked her few belongings.

Her body, broken with grief, collapsed on a bed from which she would never rise. Despite Aunt Helen's efforts, Tessie had given up on life. She refused food and water and quickly wasted away.

One afternoon, as Aunt Helen peeked into the room to check on her, Tessie's essence was already gone. All that was left of the woman I once called Mom was an empty earthen shell.

As Aunt Helen brought the past to life, she produced Tessie's death certificate, her tattered address book, and favorite perfume. That was all that was left of her.

Just a whiff of that perfume and I felt like I was transported back to being a little boy by Tessie's side. I could almost feel her next to me. The scent carried me to my childhood, to Tessie's funeral, to her grave. Tears poured down my face as I felt sadness and anger bubble up from within.

I was not angry at Tessie. I finally saw her for the broken woman she was. But I was angry. Angry that she was not there when I needed her. Angry that I never knew my mother's love. Angry that the man she trusted betrayed her. Angry that she was gone having never found love. And I was angry that she would never see the man I had become—educated, successful, loved and loving. And that she would never hear my or my sisters' children call her Grandma.

A little boy inside of me still longed for his mother's love. Angry. Hurt. My heart broke all over again.

Tessie's death certificate indicated that she died from respiratory arrest and myasthenia gravis—an autoimmune neuromuscular disease that causes weakness in the skeletal muscles responsible for functions involving breathing, moving arms and legs, and any of the muscles under one's voluntary control. While the root causes of myasthenia gravis are unknown, it can develop in someone with the HIV virus.

Years after I found the Grant family, I reconnected with Bobby's ex-wife. Without mincing words, she told me that

MORE THAN A WHORE

Michael Owens lived on the down-low and was the one who infected Tessie. Given her and Michael's licentious lifestyle, it is not surprising that her immune system was compromised, leading to her death.

The morning after the family reunion, while others were still asleep, Elena snuck me out of the house.

"You need to visit her," she said.

"Visit who?"

"Tessie."

The cemetery where she was buried was only minutes from Aunt Helen's house. Days before, this would have made no sense to me. Why go to a cemetery? There were only the dead. What could I possibly find there? Now, it suddenly made sense.

Placing flowers on Tessie's grave, I knelt. In that instant I was no longer a grown man at her grave. I was a ten-year-old version of myself. I was saying goodbye to my mother for the last time, and in a way I could not have fifteen years prior. My chest convulsed with sobs as I finally allowed myself to feel.

"Mom, this is Dee," I said. "I love you. I remember you. I miss you. I wish you had stayed. I wish you had fought for us. I wish you had fought for yourself. I wish you didn't have to leave this way. If you were here, you would have seen the man I've become. You and I might have had a relationship."

As my heart released the pain and anger of my turbulent life with and after Tessie, I felt whole. My life was no longer shrouded in mystery. I was no longer a child so scared of my surroundings that I would be found sleeping under a dinner table in search of safety. I was now a man with a choice to forgive, to accept what was, and to let go of the past.

And Tessie ... she was no longer a whore, who, like a cuckoo, abandoned her little ones to be raised by others. She was a woman who was lost, confused, and hurting. She was my Mom. I still did not understand her choices, but I was open to allowing compassion to warm my heart toward her.

I stood up. Etoy had found and joined me at Tessie's grave. I pulled her in—my flesh and blood. I would never let her go. Holding each other as we did not have a chance to fifteen years prior, without words, we cried. And with each tear we grew closer.

I finally had closure and the answers I was looking for. I met my father and his clan. My mother and her folk. I still could not mentally or emotionally process how none of them ever came looking for us. They assumed that Kat and I were better off where we were. While I might never understand their choices, I chose to accept them. I knew that they loved me in their own way.

Feeling reborn, the gaping holes in my heart patched up, I was ready to begin the next chapter of my life.

LIKE A SCAB
I WANTED TO
PEEL HIS
IDENTITY OFF ME.

TWENTY-TWO

A NAME OF MY OWN

By Thanksgiving of the same year, Edward Sr. was released from prison. The honeymoon of finding him and the rest of the family had worn off. It was time to meet him face to face to ask the hard questions that hadn't been answered yet. I wanted a man-to-man conversation.

Edward Sr. was a shell of the man he once was. Three heart attacks and two strokes made it difficult to communicate with him. He was partially paralyzed, dragging his body when he walked and slurring his words when he spoke. Although in his fifties, Edward was far from being a man. He was an underdeveloped man-child. Far from brilliant, most of his conversations revolved around women and material things.

However, I knew that my memories of him were not a figment of my scarred childhood brain. I had to hear for myself about the abuse we suffered at his hand.

To get some alone time, Elena and I took him out. He picked his favorite place: Red Lobster. Handicap be damned, within minutes Edward was flirting with our waitress, who was young enough to be his daughter. With winks and head nods he encouraged me to do the same, as if unaware that Elena was there.

With the meal warming his belly, I tackled my questions one by one.

Why did you try to kill me?

Why didn't you come looking for us after we were taken from you?

Why did you molest your daughter?

With each question, like a threatened turtle, he retreated deeper into his shell, looking scared and pitiful. I was no longer a helpless boy, seconds away from suffocating at his hand. He was no longer in charge. Pathetic and shriveled up, he denied everything. Having gotten to know him, I knew it wasn't because truth hurt. It was a survival response. He was protecting himself. Rather than answering my questions, he told me about Tessie—how she was unfaithful to him, and how she aborted his children. Just like that, he was the victim.

Shame was not in his vocabulary. By the end of the day he even asked me to buy him shoes. Edward was not even a tenth of the man John Brown was. I would never call him Dad again. As far as I was concerned, the only father I had was the man who raised me.

If there was one purpose our trip served, it was to solidify the fact that by grace and mercy, as painful as my childhood was, I was better off away from this man. Had I stayed in his care, if I survived his abuse, I might have turned out like him or, worse yet, like my half-brother.

After this trip my contact with Edward was sporadic

and infrequent. There was not much for us to talk about. And when we spoke, he got upset every time I called him Edward instead of Dad. One time it was worse than usual—tempers flared and he hung up on me. Months later he called to apologize.

We had no further contact until, years later, I received a call from his sister. Edward was hospitalized, having suffered his latest heart attack. He was dying. I asked her to put the receiver to his ear and spoke my peace.

"I wished I had known you better. I wish you were a better father than you were. But I cannot hold your past against you. I pray that we meet again in the afterlife. For now, you can go in peace. I forgive you."

A day later he was no more. His body was cremated. Grandma offered Kat and me the ashes. We both declined. There was nothing of this man that I wanted to keep. His DNA coursing through my veins was more than enough.

Years later on her deathbed, Edward's sister, my aunt, reached out and gave me carte blanche to anything I wanted to know about him. My worst memories were not the worst of what she told me. He was not only a serial rapist and a pedophile who attempted to kill me and sexually assaulted my innocent sister on numerous occasions, but he also raped all of his sisters and nieces. Even right before his death he was accused of yet another sexual assault against a mentally handicapped woman.

This planet was better off without him. I only prayed that he had a moment of repentance before taking his last breath. I no longer bore any resentment toward him, nor a desire for him to have been a better father to Kat and me. He played his role in my life. That was enough.

However, I did not want to continue his legacy. Like a scab I wanted to peel his identity off me. Like filthy rags, I wanted to tear it off and have no further association with anything of his. I used to think that it was my purpose to redeem the Wilkins name. But there came a time when I knew that it was neither my duty nor responsibility and that his name did not deserve to live on.

So, after years of bearing the name of a man who did not deserve the right to be called my father, I decided to pick a name for myself. It would have to be a name that I could cherish and proudly pass on to my children and my grandchildren. And it would have to be a name that my family would be proud to bear.

So, after multiple family discussions and searching through every language available through Google, we settled on Isoldi. Isoldi means wealth and money in Italian. For a boy who grew up poor and destitute, *isoldi* has a special meaning. Demetrye Isoldi—a person who would never allow past fears of poverty and brokenness to overshadow his thirst for life, his happiness, and his joy.

Demetrye Isoldi. It has a ring to it.

In the meantime, thanks to Elena's constant encouragement, I reestablished my relationship with the Browns. When I set out on my quest to find my roots, our relationship suffered greatly. I felt betrayed by them and was ready to cut them off. If it weren't for Elena, I would have deleted their numbers and erased my childhood home address from my memory, but she wouldn't let me.

I held onto my hurt for a while, but even volcanoes settle after an eruption. All I needed was to meet my biological family, time to synthesize what happened, and a willingness to see the Browns' side of the story.

I know that I am not the only adopted child who's had a desire to reconnect with blood relatives. I could see that they were not the only adoptive family who was scared about possible outcomes. My desire was a threat, an undermining of their efforts and love for me. They felt betrayed and scared. And if there is one thing I learned, it was that you cannot reason with a heart. You must give it time and be willing to understand it.

Months had passed since I found the Wilkinses and the Grants. My heart was softening. One day Anne reached out unexpectedly.

"If I had ever done anything to hurt you, Dee," she said, "I'm sorry. I did the best I could."

This was the closest she ever came to apologizing for all the pain she inflicted on me, but it was all that it took to bring us back together.

Having visited the dysfunction I could have been raised in, I had a deeper appreciation for what I was given by life, flawed as it was—the Brown family. I finally understood that while there was no excuse for abuse, it was no easy feat to take in two children with such a traumatic background. Right or wrong, they gave us all they possessed. We were no angels. They were no demons. We and they were broken, and we gave this love of ours our best shot.

I reconciled with Anne and profusely apologized to my parents for the hell I put them through growing up. A few years later, when Mom and Pop passed (Mom from breast and ovarian cancer and Dad from dementia and old age), I had nothing but gratitude in my heart toward them. They were my true parents when I bade my final farewell.

I NOW STOOD TALL
AND CONFIDENT,
READY TO OFFER MY
INPUT AND
CHANGE THE
WORLD AROUND ME.

TWENTY-THREE

A LEGACY OF MY OWN MAKING

WHILE SOME kids inherit their parents' strengths or legacy, my multiple parental figures left me with something no kid wishes for when blowing out his birthday candles—pain and insecurities, trauma and self-loathing.

My mother didn't want me. Both my father and my mother tried to kill me. My adopted father, a good man in comparison to my sperm donor, had a hard time expressing love. During our entire time together, before his passing, he said "I love you" to me only twice. Once when I was twenty and another time when I was twenty-one. Each of these times, I stopped everything I was doing, boarded a Greyhound bus and went to see him.

His "I love you" meant more than this world to me. Most of my childhood his favorite expression for me was: "What are you, stupid?" It was akin to having a nickname—WhatAreYouStupid Demetrye. Hear this long enough and you begin to embody it. Even in my thirties, already a married man, I would have to work hard to shake off the feeling of inadequacy, as Pop's "What are you stupid?" would flash through my subconscious mind.

My adopted mother was hands off. She already raised her flesh and blood kids. I was Anne's responsibility. By all rights, Anne should have been the one I called Mom. Liza, not a violent person, did not bother intervening when Anne beat me senseless. Her favorite response to each of my requests was "No!" I felt that it was her way of saying that I cannot be trusted in making my decisions, big or small.

And, of course, Anne—the woman I loved and feared. A mother in deed but not in name. She was skilled in taking me to the brink of unconsciousness, only to shower me with love afterward. She taught me that kids are to be seen but not heard or trusted.

While most kids have two parents, I had five: Tessie, Liza, Anne, Edward, and John.

Tessie, Liza, and Anne—to whom I would compare all women I meet for years to come, looking for the same shortcomings and transgressions in their character in order to validate the narrative they caused me to create about women in my mind.

Edward and John—the men who were supposed to teach me how to be a man, yet failed, as one was a criminal and an abusive man-child and the other, a kind-hearted, emotionally constipated workaholic who could not say "I love you."

Each of my parental figures created insecurities and brokenness in me that would last a lifetime and nearly cost me everything. Hurt or be hurt, not to be trusted with making decisions, WhatAreYouStupid Demetrye was not ready to enter the world of independence when he turned nineteen. Yet he did.

A LEGACY OF MY OWN MAKING

The legacy I received from my parents was shattered self-esteem, which would haunt me well into my twenties, compromising every opportunity and every relationship. It would take me years to start breaking through the beliefs I formed in my childhood. In the meantime, I was making a million mistakes, hoping to pay for none.

And then I met her. The one that would change it all for me. But not without paying dearly for it.

Elena. She could see beyond my screw-ups and limitations. "What was" was not as important to her as "what can be." Each day is a new possibility. Each day is filled with grace. Each day she lived by:

Treat a man as he is and he will remain as he is. Treat a man as he can and should be, and he will become as he can and should be.
Johann von Goethe

The quote was taped to her work computer screen. Each time I came to see her I saw it, but at that time I did not fully understand its meaning. However, the more time I spent with Elena, the more it sank in. Slowly, as if with a fishhook, moving at the speed of my trust, Elena began to pull giftings and talents out of me that I did not know were there.

"What are your dreams, Demetrye? Your biggest, scariest, wildest dreams?" she would ask.

I had dreams. They were seeded on my first trip to Disney World. But no one asked me about them before. I had been told what to think, what to feel, and how to live but never asked what I wanted from my life. Now life presented me with an opportunity to vocalize my dreams and even upgrade them. It would be up to me to figure out a way to materialize them.

"ANYTHING is possible," Elena believed. "If you can

imagine it, you can make it happen."

So I began to dream bigger. To think beyond my ingrained limitations. With fear and trepidation, I started to believe that this boy from New Jersey might amount to something big after all and even fulfill his childhood dreams.

Elena got me into her favorite pastime—reading. A voracious reader, she introduced me to every bookstore in town and online until I became addicted to reading and thinking for myself, independent of the beliefs that were deeply ingrained in me by others.

History, biographies, politics, spiritual, and mindset categories quickly became my favorites. I was introduced to a world of new possibilities. The world changers and thought leaders I read about often came from equally obscure and traumatic beginnings as mine. If they could make it to become leaders, business owners, millionaires, billionaires, and change the social climate of the world, the only thing that would keep me from doing the same would be me.

My mind changed. My speech changed. My behavior began to change. The way I thought about myself began to shift. I no longer shriveled up in fear if a supervisor called me into his office, scared it would be to reprimand me. I now stood tall and confident, ready to offer my input and change the world around me.

While retraining my brain was not an overnight process, I was slowly upgrading my belief system. The transformation began when I left for college. I spent time with people who weren't like me. I made friends with people from Russia to Illinois, from Israel to Wisconsin, from Brazil to Puerto Rico. My inner world began to shift. When I met Elena, the transformation became more intentional. Everything I read and everything we talked about brought me closer to

A LEGACY OF MY OWN MAKING

materializing the dreams I was brave enough to dream.

I began to question my upbringing. The beatings, the shaming—were they necessary like I had thought? Could you raise a child without "spare the rod and spoil the child" approach? How was it that Elena and her family turned out better than I did, having suffered less than one-thousandth of the "discipline" I had to survive? My beloved Black community took pride in how they handled discipline. I was raised to believe that beatings were good for me. "Look at where those beatings got you, boy. You aren't in prison. Not dealing drugs. You aren't dead. It paid off!" They wanted me to be grateful for their violence.

If violence worked, then why did it create more violence? Mom and Pop abused their kids, calling it discipline. Anne abused Kat and me, under the same guise. Bobby abused his wife. Roger sexually abused Kat. Violence did not create better outcomes for any of us. Yet beatings, verbal abuse, humiliation—true Jim Crow tactics, now strongly instilled into the African American community, became our identity so much so that when I stood up to challenge it, Anne told me: "You were influenced by the White people too much, Dee."

It was as if the ripple effects of slavery, the beatings, punishments, humiliation, lynching, and separation of families became a part of our DNA and we would defend them rather than separate ourselves to become the fierce, independent people we once were before slave ships whisked our ancestors away to shackle their bodies and their spirits.

Spanked only twice in her entire life by her father, Elena could not wrap her mind around the discipline tactics used on me, such humiliation as naked beatings.

Once we visited an all Black church in Pennsylvania.

While other congregations ended their services with praise reports and prayer requests, in this one, the service ended in a public shaming of a ten-year old boy for misbehaving in school.

"Bring him up here, sister Amy," said the pastor to his mother.

What was to follow made Elena boil with indignation until she could take it no more and walked out of the building. The boy was shamed in front of the entire church and promised a public flagging if he did not get his act together.

"Hurt people hurt people," Elena would often say. "No one can withstand such public shaming without being affected."

Was this true? Or was I being swayed by a different worldview? A lifetime, along with multiple generations' worth of beliefs were being challenged. Would I have turned out better if I were praised rather than beaten? Admonished rather than shamed? How far could I have gone with my life if I removed all childhood limitations from myself? Could Edward and his son have become something other than rapists and a murderer if their parents did not generationally propagate violence under the guise of discipline?

My grandfather Henry, Edward's father, was notorious for beating his kids senseless, boys and girls alike. The kids became numb, thinking that this is what love and parenting should feel like, and were used to violence more than love. Their mother—scared and silent to intervene, or, perhaps, agreeing with such measures, was a passive abuser.

Dysfunction abounded among Henry and Pearl's kids and grandkids—parenting children by multiple women, raising sexually abusive progenies, a rapist and a murderer, and a drug addict; uncles molesting their nieces. Atrocities that would make your skin crawl.

A LEGACY OF MY OWN MAKING

Do beatings really equate to discipline? Does such discipline translate to raising better quality people? Because if that were true, the Wilkins children should have turned out to be the most upstanding citizens. However, that was not the case.

The more enlightened I became, like fish rescued out of a swamp and placed into fresh waters, I could finally breathe and think for myself. I knew that the answer was "No!" Violence does not produce greatness. And I knew that by the time I had kids of my own, I would be a transformed man. I was not going to pass this dysfunction down yet another generation. I knew that I would have to trust and learn from my wife on how to become a parent whose legacy is love and prosperity, not brokenness.

However, the changes I dreamt about did not happen overnight. My brokenness was about to cost me everything I held dear.

PART FIVE

FREEDOM HAS A COST

I WAS WILLING
TO GAMBLE MY
MARRIAGE, HER
HEART, AND
MY FUTURE TO
SATISFY MY
FANTASY.

TWENTY-FOUR

POINT OF NO RETURN

"Do you know what love is Demetrye?"

"No, but I am willing to learn if you show me," I told her after asking her to spend the rest of her life with me.

It did not happen overnight, but something made this woman, who was way out of my league, fall for me. I don't think she could tell you what it was if you asked her. "Because you are you," she would tell me when I inquired.

Together, we decided we would defy the expected and instead of growing colder toward each other the longer we were married, we would fall even more in love each year we shared.

"It will require a lot of work and commitment," Elena said. "I am committed if you are."

Of course I was! I had no clue what to expect from marriage, but I had this shining dream in Elena that I did not want to part with. To keep her, I was willing to commit to walking on broken glass if I had to.

When I first met her, true, deep, exhilarating love lodged deep into my defective DNA, threatening to change everything I was programmed to be. I welcomed the possibility. The fear of my past was ever-present, but I thought that my love for Elena was the force I needed to deliver me from my struggles. I was too naïve to understand that love and hoping alone cannot make a meaningful transformation possible. Me hoping we would last as my addictions would fade away on their own would turn out to be a fantasy. Praying that my dysfunction would not mire her purity would be a dream not meant to materialize.

Elena was not so naïve. While she could not predict the future, she knew we both would have to put work into creating a marriage we committed to. She was aware that I came with baggage. And she knew my heart. "For better or for worse, 'til death do us part." She was all in.

Before saying "I Do's," we committed to abide by one rule in our relationship: "naked and not ashamed." While we were physically both beautiful naked, the nakedness we committed to was that of heart and soul.

"No secrets!" Elena said. "I can forgive a lot of things, but I cannot forgive a betrayal."

I knew she meant it. I had seen her with others. Always loyal and long-suffering. She could forgive and work through almost anything, but a betrayal, while she could forgive, she would not condone. She would let go of the people who betrayed her, wishing them nothing but the best. She never said anything negative about them, but never put herself in the same situation twice. I did not want to find out how it felt to be without her if I pushed her too far.

"No secrets! I want the truth. You can tell me anything that happened before me," she said. "And any temptation that you face while with me. As long as you are faithful, I will be there for you."

I cannot say that the openness and honesty she requested were easy for me. I was ashamed. Always ashamed. I would have rather lied than told her the truth. But I was a horrible liar and she was a human lie detector. What I did not share, she eventually figured out. So, I told her of my temptations, of my struggles, and of (almost) all my perverse desires, hoping that my love for her would be enough to keep me faithful. But the talons of my past were still deeply embedded in my soul, threatening to destroy the life we were creating. I was stuck in internal struggle, torn between two worlds—love versus addiction, loyalty versus compulsion.

As I was fighting for my marriage, the hidden parts of my old nature were drawing me back. I was torn between the life I was building and my secret self. Since childhood, my subconscious was programmed to expect and accept rejection. So unconsciously, I kept pushing the boundaries, testing the limits of Elena's grace to prove to myself that all women are alike. It seemed that I was set on hurting her before she could hurt me.

It puzzles me as to why, but she endured. She kept reminding me that she was not my mother or sister, and that she loved me just as I was. I did not have to do anything to prove to her that I was worthy of her love. In her, as long as I did not act on my urges, I had support and, often, guidance. If she did not feel she could help, she was always on the lookout for a mentor or a book for me.

She bore my darkest secrets. Patiently. All on her own. Always protecting me. Never revealing my shame to another soul. She stayed committed and faithful to me, body and heart. However, against my better judgement, I failed to do the same ...

February of 2006, nearly four years into our marriage I pushed Elena to the point of no return.

Now living back in Ohio, one evening we got a dreaded call—Elena's father, who suffered from Parkinson's, was on his deathbed.

"Baby, come home if you want to say goodbye," her mother told her.

The next day we were on a flight out. The day after, having held out to say goodbye to his children who flew in from all corners of the country, Elena's father took his last breath. She was there to see him off.

A few days after the funeral, we were home. My wife was plastered on the couch for three days straight—a severe case of flu topped by grief. She could not keep down any food or water. She slid in and out of consciousness. Stricken with grief and pain, she pushed through.

But I did not.

I suffered from angina (severe chest pains) and high cholesterol. While recovering and still grieving, Elena got busy looking for doctors for me. Cancers, strokes, and heart attacks ran rampant in my biological family. She could not stand the thought of losing another man she loved and the love of her life.

Test after test. Doctor after doctor. Nothing came up. And then ... Hades himself possessed me.

After yet another appointment, while Elena was at work, I found myself driving on the wrong side of town. Like a hungry wolf, I searched. For what? I wanted an experience I was too ashamed to admit to my wife. An experience that had been bubbling up to the surface from the depths of my distorted desires. Too possessed to think clearly, the thought of hurting and losing Elena did not even enter my mind. I was willing to gamble my marriage, her heart, and my future to satisfy my fantasy. So, I searched until I found what I was looking for.

I committed the only thing from which there was no return—betrayal. Betrayal of her trust. Her love. Her confidence in me. Betrayal of the heart that only knew loyalty. Betrayal of the only person that saw in me that which I was too blind to recognize in myself.

In our culture, we brush off infidelity, as if it is no big deal. Around forty percent of marriages in America end up in divorce due to infidelity. Roughly fifty percent of unfaithful partners stay married. And because they do, we assume that people can move on, they can get over the pain, and we think infidelity is okay. However, I had learned the hard way that not everyone gets over the pain. Not everyone moves on. If they do, they are not the same person they were before. Betrayal, on such a deep and personal level, changes people. It breaks their soul as deeply as abuse had broken mine.

Elena's pure heart that loved me through the hardest times of my life and gave me the best moments was about to be shattered into a million pieces. She was about to move into the zip code of Hell, and I was the responsible party for moving her there.

My fantasy was fulfilled. As if coming out of a drug induced stupor, immediately, I felt like the scum of the earth. Reality sank in. She asked me for loyalty. I gave her betrayal. She gave me love. I gave her pain. When she needed me the most, in the time of grieving over her father's passing, I repaid her with the brokenness of my charred soul.

I tried to hide my wrongdoing. I tried to bury my guilt. But you can hide nothing from her. She is a human K-9. As we laid in bed that night, naked, she turned to me for comfort. The pain of losing her father was still raw. She looked at me and ...

She knew.

I could see it in her face. Before I could say a word, I saw her age in front of my eyes. I saw her innocence stripped away. Her trust betrayed. Her breath knocked out of her lungs.

"Demetrye, tell me that you didn't! Please tell me that you didn't!" she pleaded, moving away from me with each word she barely whispered, horror washing over her lovely face, tears welling up in her lovely green eyes.

I could not lie to her.

So, I laid there. Naked. Ashamed. Wishing to vanish. Like Adam, hiding from God's presence. Wishing that she loved another instead of me. Wishing her the love she deserved, which was not mine.

As I watched the pain charcoal her soul, innocence snuffed out of her, I confessed.

Betrayal was one thing she could not forgive. I knew it. She knew it too. She was also a person of her word. Confessed, I knew that there was no coming back from what I did.

She pressed me for details to make sense of what happened to her and why. I resisted. But I could not deny her the truth. Pain added to her grief. Like nails into Christ's hands, I crucified my wife that night and then pierced her side.

Always a fair person, instead of kicking me out, she packed a suitcase and left. Hours passed. Dozens of text messages from me —"Just tell me that you're okay."—before I would hear from her.

When she stepped back through the door of our apartment that night, where every piece of furniture and decoration was lovingly placed by her two hands, she came back as a woman I had never met. People do not come back from betrayal unchanged. The Elena I knew and fell in love with was dead. I witnessed a corpse in human flesh stand in front of me. Ashen from grief. Changed forever. Eerily, with each word measured out, she spoke.

"I do not know what I will do tomorrow. Tonight, I am going to stay in MY place. You can have the bedroom."

And that was it.

Day after day passed. I was too scared to ask, too ashamed to approach her. I watched her go through her day, as if a mechanically wound clock. Up for work, lunch prepared, out the door. Done with work, back home, house cleaned, dinner served.

She was in pain. But, too callous after a lifetime of neglect, pain and abuse, I failed to understand the depth of her suffering. I wanted her to get over her pain, like I got over mine so many times throughout the years. I wanted her to love me, as if nothing happened, the way I loved my abusers and even justified their wrongdoing. I wanted her to be angry with me, to yell at me, to punish me. I wanted her to tell the whole world about my sin against her. But she wouldn't give me the satisfaction. I wanted her to move on. What's the big deal? It happened only once!

I wanted her to be the woman I fell in love with. But ...

People do not come back from betrayal unchanged, no matter how many excuses we make, or how we paint the story to soothe our guilty, broken souls.

The Bible says in Ezekiel 37:

The hand of the Lord was upon me, and he brought me out by the Spirit of the Lord and set me in the middle of a valley; it was full of bones. He led me back and forth among them, and I saw a great many bones on the floor of the valley, bones that were very dry.

My Elena, my heart and my soul, my very reason for existence, the woman who saw the world in me before I could see it myself, was gone. She became the valley of dry bones ... at my hand.

Her "I love you's" ceased, and my soul became a parched land. I longed for her voice, for her touch, for her intimate gaze. I longed for "You can do anything you can imagine." I longed to be naked and not ashamed with her.

In the words of Dante Gabriel Rossetti, 18th century English poet, I felt like a desolate land without her.

> *What of her glass without her? The blank grey*
> *There where the pool is blind of the moon's face.*
> *Her dress without her? The tossed empty space*
> *Of cloud-rack whence the moon has passed away.*
> *Her paths without her? Day's appointed sway*
> *Usurped by desolate night. Her pillowed place*
> *Without her? Tears, ah me! For love's good grace,*
> *And cold forgetfulness of night or day.*
> *What of the heart without her? Nay, poor heart,*
> *Of thee what word remains ere speech be still?*
> *A wayfarer by barren ways and chill,*
> *Steep ways and weary, without her thou art,*
> *Where the long cloud, the long wood's counterpart,*
> *Sheds doubled up darkness up the laboring hill.*

Elena knew me better than I knew myself. When I betrayed her, I lost my compass. I lost my world. For a piece of a fleshly coin, I became her judge, her jury, and her executioner.

People do not come back from betrayal unchanged. Fool ourselves as we might, they simply do not. Even if they stay and their bodies might be with us, their souls vanish. We might try to glue the pieces of their broken hearts back together, but, like a broken vase, the cracks will always be there.

Too ashamed to beg for mercy, too scared to leave, I waited. Whatever she decided, I would have to abide by it.

The day of reckoning finally came. Elena's ghost walked through the door and placed Dissolution of Marriage papers on the dinner table.

"Look through it," she said. "I think I was fair. We can split everything. Or you can take it all. I do not care.

"I do not think we need a judge. We can do mediation. All you have to do is read through it and sign."

The day of reckoning was upon me. The debts were called in. I buckled at the knees, almost too faint to stand. Reality sunk in.

"Okay," was all I could squeeze out of my throat, tears pouring down my terrified face.

Elena, still being true to herself, told no one about my misdeed. She made a covenant in our marriage to never air our dirty laundry and she lived by her commitment, suffering silently.

"It's between you and me. No one else needs to judge you," she told me.

I marveled. How could this be possible? When I went through the worst of it with Tracy, she told the whole world a lie about me to vindicate herself. Yet here was a woman who had no guile or guilt, willing to bury my shame under her tombstone. "No one needs to know."

I begged and pleaded with her. "Tell the world. Tell them, Elena!" I knew I deserved the punishment. I longed for it. It would be a welcomed reprieve from her refusal to belittle and humiliate me. If she did, I would be proven right—all women are the same. But she refused.

I looked at the paperwork. She asked for nothing. Not that I had much to give.

"All that I ever wanted from this relationship, Demetrye, was you," she told me.

That was the only thing I failed to give her.

I WAS WILLING TO PROMISE WHATEVER IT TOOK TO KEEP HER IN MY LIFE WHILE SHE WAS WILLING TO LIVE ALONE IN HER PAIN, TO KEEP MY DIRTY SECRET CONCEALED.

TWENTY-FIVE

ONE DAY AT A TIME

REGRET SET in. But now it was too late. Like a bull in a china shop, I had my way in her life and now I had to watch the aftermath.

I saw her fade away. The thought that I was the cause of this paralyzed me. I knew she should abandon me, but deep in my soul I silently pleaded with her and the heavens for a chance to stay.

For five years, since meeting her, I tried to behave. For five years I battled with myself. For five years I forced myself to be better for her. For five years she told me, "Demetrye, do it for yourself, not for me. Even if I am not in your life, you need to be free for yourself." This is what I sacrificed the day I stopped denying my broken nature.

Was it to satisfy my flesh? My desires? Or was it to hurt her before she, like all other women in my life, would end up hurting me? I could not tell you. I was a man possessed.

In a last-ditch effort, I asked, "Can we try counseling?"

"Why?" she asked. "You cannot undo what has been done. However, if you need to do it to make yourself feel better, sure, I will do it for you. Once."

So, I scheduled an appointment with a pastor of the church we began to attend only a couple of months prior. He did not even know us. But I was willing to bare my shame to a stranger for a chance to fix the unfixable.

The day arrived. We were seated at Pastor Jim's office. Ashamed, I told him the reason for our visit. He listened patiently. It was apparent that mine was not the first story of infidelity he heard. As I finished, as if asking for the wrath of God ...

"But it happened only once," I said.

Elena's body twisted in my direction. Pain contorted her lovely features. I was about to face off with a wounded lioness.

"Only once? Because that, somehow, makes it easier? More justified?" she asked.

The moment I said it, I knew that I had scales over my eyes this entire time, justifying my sin to myself to lessen the pain of my guilt. She was right. Once or twenty times, it did not matter. Not to Elena. And, if I were honest, not to me.

After what seemed like an hour-long pause, pastor Jim spoke.

"Tell me what you think, Elena."

"Besides this weakness of his," she responded, her anguish visible, "he is an amazing man. I cannot take that away from him."

Pastor Jim sat stunned. If my sin was not first of a kind for him, it looked like Elena's response was. At least it must have been unusual. He asked to clarify. She repeated herself tearfully, honestly, able to separate me from the evil I had done. In her pain, she was able to evaluate the situation objectively, without letting her pain cloud her judgement. She saw the man and his deed as separate, not the same.

I was shocked. How was this possible? I caused her so much pain and here she was, free to humiliate me, yet she showed mercy. What have I done?

Pastor Jim looked at me.

"I've done this for over twenty years, Demetrye," he said. "But I had never heard a response like this. Normally pain clouds reason and people tear each other to pieces. You are a blessed man."

Blessed? I don't know if I could call myself that. Lucky? Not even close. Surprised? I shouldn't be. But I was. She wouldn't give me the one thing I deserved the most—a punishment. It was almost as if she was incapable of it.

By the end of the appointment Elena was clear—if I wanted to do counseling, I would have to do it on my own. This would be the first and the only time she would open her wounds and her shame to anyone outside our marriage.

"If you must, you have to figure it out. I am done. I did not ask for it. Did not cause it. I will not be digging you out of your mess this time. Time to grow up, Demetrye."

Succinct and straight to the point. True to her nature. She had done nothing to push me toward what I did. This was about me and me alone.

So, one day at a time, paperwork awaiting my signature, making no promises, she stayed. Each day free to shame me. Each day free to leave me. Each day staring in the face of her executioner.

"People get over infidelity," some say. I wanted to believe it, because that could, somehow, absolve my sins and warrant me to do what I wanted, or at least to expect her to get over the betrayal, as if nothing happened.

"People get over infidelity." Perhaps it is a lie we tell ourselves so we would not feel the depth of shame and pain we inflict on those who love us. Perhaps our souls got culturally conditioned, charred in the pursuit of personal pleasure so much that we made up this bulls**t story to pacify ourselves.

But what I found from experience is that it's pure rubbish. Just as one cannot unsee the horrors of war or "just get over" physical or emotional abuse, one cannot un-feel the damaging pain of intimate betrayal.

When she chose to stay with me, one day at a time, I hoped that we could go back to the way things were. Little did I know that it was no longer her who stayed. It was a broken replica of her from a parallel universe. The woman I fell madly in love with was gone. Forever. The only time I would ever get a glimpse of her again would be when we welcomed our child into this world. Those unadulterated moments they shared were when I would see the woman who loved me deeply and innocently before I unleashed the hordes of hell to violate her pure soul. It would take years for me to earn her trust again and for us to move beyond the pain.

Years later, when I asked her why she stayed, Elena told me.

"I could not tell you if I tried. With everything in me I wanted to and had the right to leave. To stay meant to lose self-respect.

"I thought that I would never allow anything like this to happen to me. I would certainly never do it again. If I were my friend or my daughter, I would tell me to run or even drag me out of such a situation. But at that time, I just knew in my gut that it wasn't the time.

"I took it one day at a time. Patching up one crack of my heart at a time. Knowing full well that our love would never be the same. And if it wasn't our love that kept us together at times, it was our pain."

She made one request of me back then, when she made the decision to stay.

"I know I will hurt. As we rebuild what has been broken, I know I will be raging like hell with fury when the pain bubbles up to the surface. I know it will happen. If you want to see if we can survive it, whether it takes a month, a year, ten years or a lifetime, you must be willing to endure my pain and live with the consequences. Can you commit to that? And can you commit to seeking your freedom for yourself this time?"

Would I? Of course, I would! Up until then, every time I tried to break free from my addictions and my brokenness, I did it for something outside of me—family, God, church, Elena. This time, I had to do it for me, not for her or anyone else. Whether she stayed or left, she wanted me to get my freedom for me, so I could live a life without guilt and regrets. Naively, however, I thought it would be easy to endure her pain and her fury because I caused it.

Years would pass, many tears will be shed, many moments of pain would trickle away before I would fully understand the commitment she asked for.

But all that is in the future. For now, I was willing to promise whatever it took to keep her in my life while she was willing to live alone in her pain, to keep my dirty secret concealed, come hell or high water.

No one, except for the people I chose to confide in, until these pages were written, ever found out the villain I was. To our friends and our family, I was a picture-perfect husband because, even at the worst moments of her pain, Elena chose not to mire my reputation.

FIVE YEARS
MARRIED, I STILL
HAD NOT LEARNED
THAT ALL SHE
WANTED WAS ME.

TWENTY-SIX

AT HER COST

SHE STAYED. Not because she was delusional. She had enough time to have become acquainted with my shortcomings and weaknesses, and the pain they caused her. She had already suffered so much since meeting me, so she was not naïve. She knew it was not going to be easy to stay because, thus far, it had not been easy to love me.

She kept me alive in more than one way until this point—seeing me through three brain surgeries, nursing me back to life after each, putting up with my broken brain, putting up with my insecurities and addictions, helping me find my family, nursing me back from cardiovascular health issues, and opening my eyes to a new world of possibilities.

She never got a chance to grieve her father's passing. I took that away from her. Now she grieved the loss of herself—her innocence and hopes. She grieved the loss of the life we committed to building together and the loss of her trust in me. She grieved the loss of the man she believed I became in the four years of our marriage and, when she could find the emotional space—the passing of her warm-hearted, kind, faithful-to-her-mother-until-his-last-breath father.

She was not delusional when she stayed. But little did she know that the freedom I craved would cost her so much more than she already willingly gave me.

As her soul became ravaged with grief, her body reciprocated. Symptom after symptom, health issues began to pile up. Having had to take care of me through my sick years had already taken a toll on her body. Now it seemed that whatever saving grace was holding it back from falling apart was removed. She suffered. Depression shrouded her bright soul. She kept it to herself, fighting silently, confiding in no one.

She searched for answers, but no doctor could give an official diagnosis. Libraries, conferences, meetings, books, specialists ... she looked everywhere. Nothing was helping her. Yet, while she was struggling, once again, the knowledge she acquired had saved my life. Much to my doctor's surprise, I reversed both angina and high cholesterol.

We survived 2006.

2007 was drawing to a close. It looked like, while still shrouded in pain, our marriage had a fighting chance.

By the end of the year, we decided it was time to try for a child. Not because a child would fix what was broken. Neither of us was delusional to put such a responsibility on a little being. We both longed for the joys of parenthood. And we had been doing our part to work through the pain. It was time to resume the life we planned in the beginning.

However, it seemed that such joy was not in the cards for us. We could not conceive.

After years of suffering and searching, Elena finally

found a doctor who confirmed her worst fears—her hormones were severely out of balance. Stress had taken a toll on her body. In a single visit she was diagnosed with hypothyroidism, a pituitary tumor, and infertility.

She was heartbroken. I was too. And I also carried the guilt of causing the stress that got her there. Her body functioned perfectly fine before I came into her life.

The doctor's prognosis was that her conditions were irreversible and she could do nothing, except medications, if we wanted to conceive. She refused to accept it. Not one to give up, Elena was ready for a new fight. Having helped me heal more than once, she was set on doing the same for herself. She knew that miracles are possible. This time she would have to create one for herself.

"Hell hath no fury like a woman scorned," the saying goes. In Elena's case it was "hell hath no fury like a woman denied what she wants." She threw herself back into research to create a miracle for herself and for us.

With what she discovered, we made major adjustments to our diet and lifestyle. Elena's health began to improve. There was still much to be desired, but things began to look promising.

At the same time, she needed to get away from the place where she endured so much pain. Logically, I agreed, but emotionally, I hated the idea. I liked where we lived. But guilt, my new master, was driving my decisions. To pacify it, I agreed to move to Washington, where Elena's family lived. Longview was a small mill town with no opportunities and very little racial diversity. I knew I would hate living there even though I loved my in-laws.

I said "Yes" to the move. Elena needed the time to heal and to grieve her father now that we were in a better place. Much like Pop Brown, I chose to show my love through deeds rather than words. I thought that this grand gesture would certainly be the proof of my undying love for her.

Five years married, I still had not learned that all she wanted was me.

We moved. However, it wasn't long before the move only added to her pain. While she reconnected with the people who surrounded her with love her entire life, I withdrew from her emotionally. I hated living there. I tried my best to put on a show for her family, since they did not know what transpired between us, but I could not fool her.

2008 was the year when the market bottomed out. Jobs were hard to find, especially in a small mill town of sixty thousand people. I took the first job I could get—a night shift forklift driver at one of the mills. A fine way to apply my college education.

Working nights was tough. While I was dealing with it mentally, my body was affected to the point that it would convulse in sleep. Elena had to wake me up to make sure I was okay. I could not last long living this way. She insisted I quit. She would support us while I found something that could bring me joy. I resisted. I was a man after all! I did not want to make her feel that I was living off her. The market, however, would soon settle the disagreement.

Among the last to be hired, I was among the first to be let go when the layoffs rolled around. My pride was injured. I had never not worked. Ever since I was fourteen years of age, I held a job. Married and unemployed was not how I imagined myself, but the town had nothing to offer.

"Follow your bliss," Elena insisted. "Do something that would stretch you and you would love doing."

So, at the worst economical time, I got a real estate license and became the only Black realtor in town. While many realtors were exiting the field or getting second jobs,

I was hoping I would take the local real estate market by storm. Long story short, it did not happen.

Meanwhile, we moved in with my mother-in-law, a saint of a woman. She raised fourteen children and had over fifty grandchildren. She had accepted me as her own very quickly.

The goal of us moving in was to help Elena's sister, Mom's primary caregiver, remodel the house. While Elena's father was alive, a lot of things in the house needed to be modified to make his life comfortable as he was wheelchair bound. Her Mom and sister were too worn out from taking care of him to even think about luxuries such as doors that were not scratched by a wheelchair.

We went to work the moment we moved in. While Pop Brown did not teach me how to be handy, I quickly learned carpentry and construction on my own. What Elena and I couldn't do by ourselves, we completed with the help of Elena's handy family members.

The house was coming along and Elena's health was improving. She had healed herself of hypothyroidism. Yet, she still could not conceive.

Fertility was not an issue in Elena's family. When describing their women, she would say, "They are like Pez dispensers. Want a candy? Push! There it is!" For us to have been married this long and not have a child was out of the norm for this fertile clan.

Elena, a private person even with her family, never shared her health struggles with anyone, just like she did not share our marital problems, and let them think what they might. But each baby shower, while a huge celebration of life that brought her joy, made her heart ache a little more and sink a little deeper.

"When is it our turn?" she would ask.

Her pain grew. For a long time, I did not even know how deep it was, but later I would learn that she spent five years in depression. A part of it was over the hell I put her through, a part over the loss of her old self, and a part over having to pay not only with her heart but also with her body and her dreams for my sins.

She would invite me into her pain at times, as she promised she would. I did my best to be there for her, but, as she perfectly described me, I was emotionally constipated. My upbringing did not set me up to be a great comforter, even if I was the one that caused the pain. When she hurt from the pain I inflicted on her, rather than drawing closer, I withdrew. Why would she want to be near me? I would spend hours agonizing and talking myself out of comforting her.

Elena spoke a different love language than me. She did not want big gestures or things. She did not need me to buy her a diamond ring or take her on a surprise vacation. Her love language was time. Time with me. My company. My touch. My loyalty. All the things that cost no money. All the things I found hard to give. It would have been easier if I could sweep her off her feet with a grand gesture, like a surprise trip to Cancun. But, no. She wanted me. But because I was emotionally constipated, when she hurt and needed me, I withdrew, which made her pain that much deeper, her depression that much stronger.

Meanwhile, I grew more impatient living in Longview. I blamed everything I could on being there. She was not blind. She saw it. She felt it. So, she offered to let me go more than once.

"You are not obligated to stay. You are free to go, Demetrye. Go, build your life in a place that makes you happy. Find a woman that can meet your emotional needs. Live out your deepest fantasies. You are free. I am not holding you back."

I felt like I was going mad. I hated staying, but I also did not know how to leave. I did not want to be the coward that ran when times got tough. Maybe if she pushed me hard enough, I would run. So, again, unconsciously I pushed her, testing the limits of her patience, while still holding on. Miserable myself, I created more misery for her.

But then, an opportunity came for me to have both of the worlds that I wanted—staying with Elena and leaving Longview.

IN THAT MOMENT, I
HAD EVERYTHING
A MAN COULD
EVER DREAM OF
AND MORE THAN I
EVER DESERVED.

TWENTY-SEVEN

HERE COMES OUR MIRACLE

EARLY IN 2010 I received the call from my aunt that Edward died. Not even sixty years of age, his dysfunctional life was cut short.

It was after his death that I learned that less than two years before his passing he impregnated the mentally handicapped woman he sexually assaulted. She had a baby girl. I had a sister—Breona.

My heart twinged in pain. I did not want her to have the life Kat and I had. I did not want her to be another victim of the Wilkins' upbringing. However, years later I will find out that, just like with Kat, me, and our half-brother, no fatherly love could be found in the shell of a human being Edward was. The incestuous pedophile would go on to commit a capital crime against his infant daughter. Just like Kat, she did not escape his insanity. The savage had sexually abused her. And just like before, justice eluded him. After only a few months in prison, he was released, and died a free man.

The moment I heard about Breona I wanted to know where she was and who was taking care of her. I learned that she was not with the family. When Edward's offense against her was uncovered, she was placed into the foster system and, by the time I learned about her existence, was up for adoption. Unaware of what got Breona placed into the system, I was angry. Why wasn't she with the family? Why didn't they reach out to me to let me know about her? Had I known the truth, it all would have made sense, but for now I had to believe what I was told—she was not with them because none of them felt they could raise her. Her mother was mentally incapable. Grandma was over seventy, too old to take care of a child. The aunts and uncles were barely making ends meet. So, I decided to do one thing I could for my flesh and blood—fight to get her.

Elena agreed. We had what it takes to give her the best life could offer. We could raise her as our own, giving her every privilege we had.

Time was of the essence since Breona was getting close to being put up for adoption, but Longview was not a great place to expedite the foster parent licensing process—something we had to go through in order to get her. So in a matter of weeks, we packed everything we had and headed back to Ohio.

We started the process. Even though blood relatives to Breona, we had to take foster care parenting classes first. The home inspection was done and interviews passed. However, no matter how fast we moved, the State of Georgia was moving faster. The woman who was fostering Breona was days away from signing the adoption papers.

We pleaded with Grandma. "Take her. You are her grandmother. They will let you. You are already in the state.

HERE COMES OUR MIRACLE

As soon as we finish the process here, you can transfer the guardianship to us."

We finally convinced her. We could exhale.

The day arrived and we were ready. I called Grandma to make the arrangements.

"I decided that I am going to keep Breona," she said.

I was angry and dumbfounded.

"What? You did not even want her! And we made an agreement—we finish the process here and you transfer her to us."

"I changed my mind. I cannot imagine not having her here," she said. "And I am too old to travel to see her in Ohio often."

Our world came to a screeching halt. For months we had imagined and accepted Breona as our own. We printed her pictures to remind us of the miracle we were about to embrace, and shared them with our family and friends so they could support us. For all intents and purposes, she was already ours. And now ... now we felt powerless. It was as if we had lost a child.

I tried to reason with Grandma but she would not have it. All logic gone, it seemed as if she planned on living forever.

"You only want her because you do not have kids of your own," she finally lashed out.

The pain cut deep. It felt as if a knife was plunged deep into our hearts and twisted.

"No, you old fool!" I wanted to scream. "I want her so she can have the life I did not have. So she can avoid your dysfunction. So she would avoid the abuse that Kat, our cousins, and I were unable to escape."

"What happens when you die, Grandma?" I asked instead.

"You can take her then."

After months of negotiations, we finally drew a line in the sand—we either get her now or not at all. Breona had already gone through enough trauma. To be abused and dragged from house to house, to feel the rejection of being unwanted is not what she deserved. We either get her now to give her the stability that she needs, and instill our values in her, or pray that Grandma lives long enough to raise her and keep her safe. Pearl did not relent. Breona was at her mercy.

For years to come, for Breona's sake, I stayed in touch with her. Right up until Grandma changed her number and cut us off.

Years would pass before we reconnected. We flew to Georgia to see them. Breona was already over ten. With Grandma over eighty, staying mostly home due to her declining health, which limited Breona's exposure to what a young girl's life should be, in a last-ditch effort, we extended an invitation to take Breona.

Now Breona's opinion would have to be considered. It was her life after all. Breona warmed up to the idea, but Grandma still could not part with her. As we said our goodbyes, I hoped that my sister's life would turn out better than mine did.

The pain of losing Breona was raw, but we could not stop living.

In 2002, after going back to college to complete my Bachelor's Degree, I dropped out because of brain surgery. It took three years to recover my full brain function. Now, with the worst of health and the hell I put my marriage through behind me, I was ready to complete my education. A year and a half is all I needed to get my degree, so I enrolled at a local university to get a BA in Business Management.

We settled into a routine. I worked and went to college.

HERE COMES OUR MIRACLE

Elena pursued new career goals. Given her own success in healing a thyroid condition, she changed her career direction, got involved in the health industry and got multiple certifications.

We still dreamt of having a child of our own. "It's not a matter of IF, it's a matter of WHEN," Elena would say with certainty that no one could argue. After all we had been through, from my healing to our marriage surviving, I had become a believer too. I knew if we wanted something badly enough we could make it happen.

To stay focused on our dream, we bought a couple of baby outfits and hung them in our closet. Each time we saw them, we would say a prayer of gratitude, as if our miracle already happened.

Elena plastered her workspace and the bathroom mirror with reminders of the impending miracle. "I am healed," read one of them. "If I can conceive it, I can manifest it," read another. I thought that even God could not argue about her getting what she had set her mind on. I had seen her get everything she ever focused her attention on, including saving my life, my shunt-free body, and my freedom from my past transgressions. Why would this be any different?

While her faith held strong, waiting was not always easy. In January of 2011, Elena told me that she needed a mental and emotional break from research and the pursuit of our miracle.

"I am not giving up, but I can't keep pushing like this," she said. "Baby or not, my life has a meaning and I still have so much to be grateful for."

Exhausted after three years of trying, praying, and waiting, she finally decided to take the medication her doctor prescribed for the pituitary tumor. Instead of feeling better however, the medication made her feel much worse. While she was nearly symptom-free until then, now she was swollen, wheezing, and unable to sleep. I questioned if having a baby justified such a sacrifice. Child or not, I did not want her to suffer. If I had to choose between having a baby or having a healthy wife, I would choose the latter any day.

After six months on medication and Elena's health rapidly declining, we decided to stop everything—medication, research, supplements, striving, and trying. Baby or not, our lives were still worth enjoying. We needed a break.

This is where most people would expect miracles to happen. You stop stressing and trying, you go to your mundane daily routine, you relax and do nothing, and ... BOOM! You are pregnant! That's what we heard from countless well-wishers over the years. "Stop trying, and it will happen." I don't know if this works for some, it certainly did not for us. The well-meaning remarks brought nothing but more pain.

We needed a break. We were tired of crying at night only to wake up in the morning to face another day of trying, striving, and hoping. The baby pursuit always was and would have to remain secondary to being healthy. Elena's wellbeing had to come first. So, we chose to stop medication and not consider infertility treatments or IVF. It did not seem like it was our path. I probably would have said yes to anything Elena wanted, and what she wanted was a healthy body, a natural conception, and a healthy pregnancy.

"It's not a matter of IF, it's a matter of WHEN," she would remind me often.

Weeks passed. Elena was off medication, nursing her body back to health. One night, while still detoxing and struggling from medication induced insomnia, she went back to researching and struck gold. She found a couple of promising studies—enough to whet her appetite and keep her going.

For the next few weeks she buried herself in research. There was a glimmer in her eyes that was unmistakable—she knew she was onto something life-changing.

September 14, 2011, as I was studying for an exam, Elena knocked on the office door.

"Yes?" I said.

She entered. There was a semi-crazed, semi-shocked look on her face.

"Baby, it happened!"

"What happened?" I looked at her quizzically.

She pulled out a small white object from behind her back and handed it to me. A pregnancy test!

"Pregnant," it read.

She said nothing, staring at me with the biggest grin I had ever seen.

"What?! Is this for real?" I stuttered.

"Yes! Yes, it is! Our WHEN has happened!" she responded with tears pouring down her face.

I did not know how to react. I cried like a baby. I pulled Elena in and held her tightly in my arms. In that moment, I had everything a man could ever dream of and more than I ever deserved.

I used to fear homelessness. I used to fear ending up in a prison. I used to fear losing my love. I used to fear myself. But I grew past that mess. I was becoming the man I could respect. And now I was given a chance to learn how to become the father I never had but always wanted.

I was excited. However, I was also a little nervous. What if my dysfunctional upbringing hinders my ability to be a good parent? What if I become the kind of parent my parents were? I felt that I neither had the skill nor the training to be a good parent. Yet, I was more than willing to step up.

While the undercurrent of fear would be there on and off for a while, I had Elena by my side. She assured me that I would make the greatest father our baby could have, and she would never let me fail.

If the first part of our marriage was filled with pain and heartache, I was determined to make the rest of our lives a living paradise. I would have to figure out how. I was scared. I was excited. But I was also very determined.

SHE WOULD BE
THE FIRST WOMAN
I WOULD NOT TRY
TO PUSH AWAY
OUT OF FEAR SHE
WOULD HURT ME
FIRST.

TWENTY-EIGHT

SAVING GRACE

I AM a Dad!

Our baby is still in the womb, but ...

I am a Dad!

I did not have to wait for my child to come out of the womb to start our relationship. I was going to get a jump-start so by the first breath this baby of mine would already know me, know how it feels to be wanted and loved. Any chance I had, I spoke to my baby. I read to my baby. I sang to my baby.

On Christmas Eve of 2011, I received the best gift—I felt my baby move. A little flutter, a tiny kick, my child was in there! Elena's belly was still too tiny to know she was pregnant. Up until this moment I had to accept by faith that I was on the fast track to fatherhood. Now, there was no doubt. I went from feeling like my child was a figment of my imagination to one hundred percent certainty that my baby was on the way.

It was REAL!

A few days later, as we visited our midwives, I got to hear my baby's heartbeat. Tiny, fast, persistent. The purest proof that our wildest dreams were made a reality.

Miracles are not only possible, they are probable.

It's not a matter of IF, it's a matter of WHEN.

Anything is possible for those who stick with it.

ANYTHING!

The evening before Mother's Day, Elena went into labor. Ever the champ, she spent the next thirty-six hours grocery shopping, prepping meals, and even helped me shop for bike parts. Contractions came and went while we were at the bike shop. Each time one came, Elena stepped away to labor through it, then went back to shopping as if nothing life-altering was happening.

As the day went on, the contractions intensified. Each one stronger than the one before. Watching my wife go through a pain so intense it would make a man pass out gave me a new appreciation for what women do for humanity. I wondered how a human being could have so much strength. No drugs. No screaming. No cussing me out like you see in so many Hollywood movies. Natural to the very end. Committed to feeling the baby come down the birth canal. Committed to being focused on the outcome, not the pain. One breath at a time.

Thirty-six hours later, in the comfort of our home, under the watchful eyes of two skillful midwives, we welcomed the miracle we spent years praying for into our lives. After her last and most excruciating push, Elena held our baby in her arms.

"Baby! My baby!" she chanted under her breath.

I was speechless for a few moments. But I had to know.

"Is it a boy or a girl?" I finally asked.

Elena was in a world of her own, staring at our baby's tiny face, lost to reality.

"I don't know. Why don't you look?" was all she could say.

Peeking under the birthing blanket, the mystery was over. IT WAS A GIRL!!!

Isabella.

Beautiful. Healthy. Puffy from nine months in the womb. All six pounds five ounces of her. She was the embodiment of perfection. I know each parent must feel this way, but that's what she was—perfection! Destined to have a life better than her father's. I prayed that she would be every bit as wonderful as her mother and every bit as funny as me.

I got to cut the umbilical cord. Then, I got to hold her in my arms while Elena was showering after her superhuman act of womanhood. Just the two of us for the first time. My eyes locked with Isabella's. She stared at me, as if she already knew who I was. Perhaps she recognized me from all the times I spent talking and singing to her while she was in the womb.

I knew that I would never be the same. I was in love. In love with this tiny being. In love so deep that I would walk into a burning building, stay up sleepless nights, and crawl on my hands and knees making baby sounds just to keep her happy.

This tiny being, this daughter of mine, had stolen my heart. She would be the first woman I would not try to push away out of fear she would hurt me first. This tiny being, with the force of the entire Universe in her, was my saving grace, my redemption, my chance to start the next chapter of my life with a clean slate.

She will not judge me for my past. She will not compare

me to others. She will not care whether I have a college degree or not. She will not reject me. She will only be interested in having the most intimate relationship a human can have with another—that of a child and parent. I swore to protect that sacred bond with my life. Isabella was guaranteed to have the best father I could form out of this pile of clay called me.

That night, we could not go to sleep. Midwives gone, Elena and I lounged on our bed admiring our miracle. Ten fingers. Ten toes. A tiny face.

We dreamt of her future. Of our life together. Of the moments of joy and the sleepless nights we knew lay ahead. We soaked in every second, enraptured in the now, as if the world outside did not exist. We were safe inside our family bubble.

PART SIX

A MAN OF MY OWN MAKING

I AM CONVINCED
THAT OUR DESTINY
IS THE OUTCOME
OF OUR BELIEFS,
OUR CHOICES,
AND HARD WORK.

TWENTY-NINE

HAPPILY EVER AFTER

IN PREPARATION for Isabella's arrival, Elena created a lifestyle that would afford her as much time as possible with our daughter. Unlike the country Elena grew up in, where women got a year-long paid maternity leave, America was and is still lagging when it comes to parenthood. Women here are lucky to get six weeks paid leave to bond with their newborns and sometimes not even that long. Fathers have it even worse. Usually no time off at all or, if lucky, a few days.

My Russian wife would have none of that. Not if she could help it. So she created a business that could thrive anywhere there was an internet connection. Nothing was going to come between her and her daughter. She never skipped a beat—pushing out Isabella at two a.m. and back to her computer, working, after waking up in the morning.

I wanted the same for myself! We waited for our daughter for so long that I wanted each moment I could get with her. I was working full-time and going to school, so time was one thing I already had very little of. I did not want to miss out on any special moments. While technology was our saving grace and I got a ton of images and videos from Elena daily, I wanted to be there with my girls.

It was time to manifest another miracle.

The university I attended had a position open not far from our house. I applied but did not get it.

"It's not a matter of IF, it's a matter of WHEN," Elena insisted once again. "You want to be with your child. Don't you?"

"Of course, I do!"

"So, apply again and again and again until they get tired of you and hire you," she told me.

A novel approach. I was going to take it.

Two months later I had my dream job—working as a recruiter.

I could work from my office or from home. If Elena ever needed anything, I was only a text message away. Special moments? I was there to witness them. Isabella's first word? I was there to hear it. First time she held her head up? I was there. First time she rolled onto her belly? I have that memory too. First crawl? I crawled next to her! Her first step? I was there to witness it.

I did not have to wish to be a better father than my fathers were. I was the kind of father my child needed—present. I read to her. I played with her. I sang to her. I bathed her. I dressed her. She slept on my chest on our rocking chair when she was sick. I went for walks with her. I was present. And I loved every single moment of it!

Still, from time to time, my fear of failing her would creep in and get the best of me. Was I really made for this? Having Elena as the mother of my child gave me comfort.

She assured me many times that I was a fantastic dad. She asked me to trust the process and to trust her lead, if that's what I needed. Her upbringing was the antidote to mine, when needed, she would reign my dysfunction in. So I had pushed my fears aside and got comfortable with learning fatherhood skills "on the job." I might not be the perfect father, if there is such a thing, but I would be all that she needed me to be to be the best father she could have.

The longer I was a father, and a human in general, the more I began to realize that perfection is elusive. It's a prison. To strive for perfection is to give up on progress and joy. But to strive for my best was to allow myself to mess up and make mistakes, to ask for forgiveness, to make things right and keep moving.

Being a father is not a destination, it's a journey. A journey that allows for detours and pit stops along the way. As Lao Tzu says in the *Tao Te Ching*: "A journey of a thousand miles begins with a single step." The day Isabella was born, I got to stepping. One foot in front of the other.

Children have a way of humbling and teaching us the lessons our adult counterparts can't because we are too proud to learn from them. So, I became my daughter's pupil. Learning, implementing, course correcting. One foot in front of the other. Each time a better version of myself.

Isabella was growing up fast. She started talking before she turned one. Her vocabulary was very rich. So rich that by the age of three she could call me out on my parenting missteps.

As her personality got to shine through more, she began to assert her individuality—a perfect reflection of me in so many ways. She challenged me and I often caught myself reacting to her the way my parents did to me. The dreaded "No" began to escape my lips more and more often. Not that

I am an opponent of all "No's," but mine were disproportionately greater compared to Elena's, often senselessly so.

"Daddy, you never let me do anything I like," Isabella would chastise me.

"You're being Liza again," Elena would tell me when I, for no reason at all, would respond with a "No" to Isabella.

Truth hurts. I did not like being compared to Mom Brown. I did not want my daughter to feel like a caged bird. So I worked harder on myself to unlearn the parenting traits I unconsciously absorbed. And not always joyfully. Who likes to face the darkness in them? But for her sake, I had to do better than was done to me.

I do not think I will ever arrive at perfection, but I will always strive to be better than the day before. One percent to infinity.

My daughter and my wife taught me that being imperfect can be good enough. This was especially true with Isabella. I learned that correcting my mistakes and apologizing for them taught her valuable lessons. If anything, she can learn from me that mistakes are a part of life. That they are an opportunity to grow. That growth is an ongoing process. That mistakes can lead to discoveries. That life is a journey of a thousand steps with a lot of detours in between.

I get to teach my daughter something that my parents did not teach me—that she can vocalize her disappointments and frustrations without the fear of punishment. In fact, we encouraged her to do just that since the time she was born so we all could grow.

One time, when she was barely three, she and I got into an argument. To discipline her, I told her to put her favorite toys away and that she won't have access to them or TV privileges for two days. She was not happy. Her tiny voice rose gradually as she stood her ground. Elena walked into the playroom, where we were, to see what we were squabbling about.

"Mommy, you can't be here right now," Isabella said, putting up her tiny hand, palm facing Elena. "Daddy and I need to talk."

"Okay," Elena responded, "but can you tell me what's going on?"

"Daddy and I need to have a family meeting," she said, making me grab her Doc McStuffins folding chair and demanding I follow her.

"Take it Daddy, and let's go to my room," she commanded.

Between her cuteness and my sheer curiosity of how this was going to play out, I followed her orders.

Shutting the door and instructing Elena not to follow, Isabella had me sit in front of her as she, for the next fifteen minutes, articulated her disappointment in my parenting skills. Any time I looked away, she would grab my face with her tiny hands, directing it toward herself, and tell me something she heard her mother say to her for three years…

"Focus on me, Daddy. Look into my eyes when I speak to you."

It was irrelevant who was right. I ended up apologizing and as is the custom in our family, we hugged it out afterward.

I am my daughter's pupil. She teaches me a lot of things—love, humility, humanity, joy, forgiveness, being lost in the moment, and never dwelling on past mistakes. And when parenting gets tough, she always reminds me that she gets her stubbornness from me and her commendable qualities from her mother.

"Daddy, when it comes to making trouble," she told me when she was seven, "you are like a huge balloon and Mommy is like a tiny fly. So, we will talk about you right now, not about Mommy."

I am my daughter's pupil. She teaches me to be the father she needs in her life. So, I became the finger-nail-painting, hair-braiding, tutu-wearing, dancing-'til-you-drop, beat-boxing, homeschooling, fly-you-to-the-moon, and loving-every-moment-of-it father. The more she teaches me, the more I learn. And these days, I say "Yes" more often than "No."

I often wonder what life would have been like if I had parents like Elena and myself. What insecurities would I not have had to deal with? What limitations would I not have had to break through? What self-doubts would I not have had to overcome?

Given, even in the best of circumstances, any of these are a part of being human. We all have insecurities, doubts, and obstacles. But not all of us have whores for mothers and rapists for fathers.

It took time, but I learned to harness what I perceived as handicaps and disadvantages of my upbringing to make me who I am today. While, like many others who suffered abuse and trauma at the hands of our guardians, I will never find out what it could be like to have parents like me and Elena, I know that if we choose to step out of the victimhood mentality, we have a chance to create whatever life we desire.

In the community I was raised in, violence was often cloaked in the guise of discipline. Parents would often brag to each other about the beatings they gave their children and how that was the reason their offspring stayed on the straight-and-narrow. Anne said on many occasions that it was her beatings that kept me out of prison.

Once she told me how she shared with a co-worker that all my accomplishments—my education, my success, me owning a house, and being happily married—were a byproduct of her discipline and parenting skills. While she could not be further from the truth, in a way she was right—my accomplishments were a byproduct of my past. But it was not her beatings and parenting skills that got me where I am today. Rather, it was my acceptance that my past, including the abuse, was a part of a divine plan. And it was me taking ownership of my past, my weaknesses, my addictions, my pain, and my ability to become the creator of my destiny that got me to become the man I am. While the heavens sent me an angel who became my saving grace not once, but twice, I was the one who had to make the choice to stop being a victim, to stop making excuses, and to become the master of my own fate.

My sisters were not so fortunate.

Kat ended up recreating an upgraded version of Tessie's life. She parented five children by four men, placing one of her daughters up for adoption. A lot like Tessie, she was always looking for the love of a man and never finding it. Always struggling to provide for her children. While her life and love choices echoed what she learned from our mother, Kat did not abandon her children. She has done whatever she could to provide for them and keep her family together.

Etoy was also not left unscathed by Tessie's legacy and experienced a similar trajectory as Kat. Given up at birth, she was raised by Sadie, Tessie's adopted mother, until she was ten. When Sadie died, a neighboring family took her in. With kids of their own, while they provided her with a roof over her head, they were not kind to her, often cruelly demeaning her for being an orphan.

By the age of twenty, Etoy became a single mother. Eventually she parented five children by three men. She, too, spent her adult life struggling financially, making ends meet, never experiencing the love I am fortunate to have in my life.

Much like Kat, she is far from being Tessie. None of her children were abandoned or have ever gone hungry. She always had a job and provided them with a roof over their heads. But she also struggled to find the love she craved.

When Etoy was going through yet another breakup at the age of forty-eight, she confided in me tearfully that she never got to discover who she really was or what it meant to be a woman. The family that raised her mistreated and humiliated her mercilessly for being motherless. She did not get to form the confidence a person needs to thrive in this world. As a result, her relationship choices always reflected her insecurities and played out the worst of her fears: you are not good enough, you are not lovable, you don't deserve happiness, you don't deserve joy, no one wants you, you will always be alone.

"All I want right now is my mother, Demetrye," she told me. "I need her to tell me who I am and what to do with my life. I need her to teach me how to be a woman. I feel like I cannot stop this vicious cycle of pain and suffering. And if you were to ask me what it is I want right now, I could not give you an answer, because I don't even know who I am."

As I reflect on how the three of us, born of the same mother, each turned out differently, I am convinced that our destiny is the outcome of our beliefs, our choices, and hard work. My heart aches for my sisters, because I believe that if they only began to challenge the lessons they learned from their guardians and pursued a mentor to guide them along their path as I did, they too could start seeing a world outside of the one in which they were raised. They too could, at any moment, choose their own beliefs. And when and if they do, they too could create a new reality.

No matter how painful it was to see the brokenness in me and bring it to light for healing, I am grateful that I chose to forge my path to life and freedom—living a life the younger version of myself would envy.

I used to be afraid of becoming a parent for fear of damaging my children or giving them the life I had. Now, instead of fear, my life is a legacy I am proud to leave for Isabella. A life that shows that we can all do better than our teachers, that we should strive to achieve more than our parents did, that we are not defined by anyone's mistakes, and that fear needs not stop us from living.

No one decides the outcomes of my life, my ability to love, my ability to be faithful, or my success except for me. The legacy I leave for Isabella is that, regardless of my dysfunctions and my violent upbringing (or maybe because of them), ultimately I get to choose the person I become. And if I can master my life, so can she. And so can you, dear reader.

THE UNIVERSE
FLUNG ITS DOORS
OPEN TO FINISH
THE MAKING
OF THE MAN
I WANTED TO
BECOME.

THIRTY

SHEDDING SKINS

I WAS many things in life—fearful, rejected, neglected, abused, guarded, a lover, and a cheater. Most of my experiences and self-identifiers landed on the negative side of the spectrum. I even believed I was meant to be a failure because I failed each time I tried to be something other than what I was at that moment.

Elena's love and faith in me, however, helped me to start seeing new possibilities. Could I be determined, accepted, loved, appreciated, appreciating, happy, respected, successful, a forgiver, and forgiven? If I could, I wanted to make it happen so I would no longer drift, rudderless, wherever my life was taking me. If I could, I would have to change my attitude. I would have to be purposeful. While I was lightyears ahead of the boy I used to be, I hadn't arrived yet. I was a work in progress! Already a father, I desired to change more.

The Universe must have heard my desire. We decided to move back to Longview, the tiny town that I loathed so much, so Isabella could be close to her family. Once again, I mourned the move, but this time I was consciously involved in the process.

"We won't move if you feel and behave the way you did last time," Elena said.

The decision was up to me. However, I could not be so selfish as to hold back her and Isabella with my hang-ups. It was time to make a conscious choice to create a new perspective of what my reality could be and live it out. So I did. I made a conscious decision to start finding joy in everything I did. The Universe, always accommodating, would ensure that I had plenty of opportunities to grow in joy and gratitude regardless of what came my way.

In the summer of 2014, we packed everything we owned and moved to Washington. While the rest of the country had recovered from The Great Recession, this town was still hurting. There were very few jobs. The higher someone's education was, the fewer opportunities were available.

It took me a month to find a job in Portland, Oregon. The drive to it was an hour long on a good day. During rush hour, it would take me up to four hours to commute. It was tough. Tough on my body and even tougher on my heart. I became the weekend parent. My daughter began to resent me because I was gone so much. This was not the dream I was hoping for. But I felt that as a man, I had to suck it up. So I did. I pushed through.

It took only a short time for the stress to catch up with me. After a year of such an insane life, I passed out on my commute to work with internal bleeding. Thankfully, I was on a transit train and surrounded by people who called an ambulance.

SHEDDING SKINS

I was hospitalized. A battery of tests and tens of thousands of dollars later, no one could tell me what was wrong. But Elena and I knew without any diagnosis that my body was telling me that it was time to change things. This life I was living was not sustainable.

We had already bought and moved into our home. Elena's business was doing very well, and we could afford for me to quit. I wanted to spend more time with my daughter and wife. I longed for a respite. Yet, due to the cultural conditioning (the man is the one who goes out to bring home the bacon), I was not yet willing to become a stay-at-home dad. For some reason, I felt that if I did, I would be less of a man. It would take me two more jobs, each closer to home, to finally realize that I could, should, and would relish that role and be as much of a man as I decided to be.

After all, it should be me, not my cultural conditioning, who defines what manhood looks like just like achieving my freedom and realizing that I was the ultimate master of my fate. Stay-at-home, work-from-home, be-at-home, or run for president—if my family and I are okay with it, that's all that matters.

The day came when I finally said "Yes" to spending more time with my daughter. "Yes" to spending more time with my wife. "Yes" to spending more time doing the things I loved. "Yes" to living the life I worked so hard to build. I finally surrendered to my desire.

As if awaiting my surrender, the Universe flung its doors open to finish the making of the man I wanted to become. I was already more successful and loved than the terror-filled young version of myself could have imagined. I had a wife, a child, a college degree, and a five-bedroom house. I was not homeless! I was not in prison. By all measures, these were great accomplishments. But something was still missing. A part of me was still broken.

Nothing happens by accident. It is through this surrender that I finalized my journey to complete freedom and found my true self.

Elena was able to fully heal her body and her heart. I watched her come back to life. Her work on herself and with her clients was mind-blowing. I saw my wife flourish, going from broken and sick to fit, happy, and healthy. She found a way to heal despite the pain she endured. She was not the same as she was before. In some ways she was better. She was stronger, more resilient, more purposeful.

Her clients came to her as broken as she used to be, and some even worse. Years of failed medical care left many maimed and hopeless. Some lost their identities, their quality of life, and their relationships to chronic health conditions. Years of suffering. They had no help from doctors and seemed to always be clinging to their last hope for a better future.

Then, in a matter of a few short months working with Elena, their lives would change. What they thought was impossible was manifesting as a reality. They would be off medications, symptom-free, rekindling their passion for life, bringing romance back into their dying relationships, starting new careers, building new businesses, becoming the parents they dreamed of being only weeks before, and loving their lives.

I was still missing something. I wanted what they were getting. So, one day I got curious and asked Elena to teach me some of the practices she used for her own healing and with her clients. She started off by teaching me the art of meditation.

One night, with Isabella sound asleep, we sat on the family room couch and she guided me through the first meditation of my life. She led me through uncovering the parts of me that still needed healing. Showed me how to quiet my mind so I could hear the voice of my past and understand what stories my body stored that still needed finishing and releasing.

I was hooked. Each day after that, I took time to meditate. I began to go deeper in my practice, bringing light to every corner of my soul that was still mired with pain and brokenness. Illuminating every inch of my being. Dealing with the shipwreck debris of my life that still needed my attention. Being honest with myself about my deepest fears, desires, and dreams.

Nothing happens by accident. Not my past. Not my pain. Not our moving to Washington. And not me quitting my job. Now that I opened the doors to a complete excavation of myself, I wanted to eradicate anything that would hold me back or set me up for an irreparable failure.

As soon as I learned meditation, Elena introduced me to the works of scientists she admired: Dr. Joe Dispenza, Dr. Bruce Lipton, Gregg Braden, Lynne McTaggart, Bessel van der Kolk, Mark Wolynn, Dr. Susan Forward, and countless others. Many of them were cutting edge neuroscientists, psychologists, and psychiatrists.

All of them had this in common: they believed that our bodies keep the memories of our past and unless we finish the emotional journey of trauma and release it from our minds and bodies, they can keep us stuck in the past. However, if we connect to a divine intelligence that resides within us, we can fully heal the pain of the past, including the emotional and physiological symptoms they cause, while retaining the memories.

One of these scientists, Dr. Dispenza, a chiropractor by training, was also a triathlete. When he was in his twenties, during one triathlon he was run over by an SUV. The accident left him with six shattered vertebrae. A large volume of shattered fragments went toward his spinal cord. He could not move and, almost immediately, ended up with a host of neurological symptoms, including several different types of pain.

In order to give him a fighting chance at walking, his doctors advised him to have spinal surgery and a Harrington rod implanted in his back. Even if the procedure was successful, he would still end up being disabled for the rest of his life. If he chose not to have surgery, paralysis was inevitable. For him, neither seemed like a great option. So, much like Elena did with my health and hers, he decided against expert medical advice.

He believed that there was an intelligence, an invisible consciousness in each person that supported, maintained, protected, and healed us in every moment. The very same force that creates almost 100 trillion specialized cells and keeps our hearts beating hundreds of thousands of times per day. He figured he could take his attention off his external world of impossibilities and instead go within and connect with this intelligence to lead to his full healing. And so he did.

It was very similar to what I saw Elena accomplish with my brain surgery, my health, and her own recovery. They might have described their processes in different terms, but the outcome was much the same.

Every day this man would connect with this intelligence while surrendering his healing to it. Nine and a half weeks after the accident, he walked back into his life—no surgeries, rods, or body casts. Fully recovered! Twelve weeks after the accident, he was back to training.

He went on to dedicate the rest of his life to studying

neuroscience and our ability to connect to the higher intelligence in us that can make even the most unlikely healing possible, from physical ailments to emotional trauma.

It seemed that my wife, Dr. Dispenza, and other great minds she introduced me to spoke the same language. Everything is possible. It's not a matter of IF, it's a matter of WHEN. If you can conceive it, you can create it. Your past does not define your future.

I dove into these philosophies. They all demonstrated, through science and practice, that if we keep reliving and replaying the past memories and emotions, for all intents and purposes we are stuck living in the past. Past pain, hurt, trauma. Past addictions, proclivities, doubts. And as long as we remain stuck, we can never fully heal and live in the present moment.

I realized that a part of me never got to grow up because, in part, I was still a little scared boy, abandoned by his mother. I was still longing for her love. I was still filled with insecurities. I was still guarded, watchful that no one hurt me. The emotions of abandonment were still in me. When they would float to the surface, I would still lash out. I was still reliving my past torments over and over, stunting my progress, keeping myself from fully enjoying the life I had built, and holding myself back from an extravagant future.

If I were to get myself to stop living in my past, perhaps I could create a whole present and future, avoiding any more destruction. I could become the creator of my life rather than the victim I had been. I could allow my life to happen for me rather than to me. And maybe, just maybe, I could make up for all the lost time. Finally, after looking for a way out of my emotional prison my entire life, I felt that I found it.

I began to work on myself daily. Often, getting up at four

in the morning to spend one to two hours in meditation while my family was still asleep. Things were changing inside of me. Things that no one but me and Elena observed. I was on my way. However, there was one more thing I would have to do to release my past and turn it into a building block of my life—earn self-forgiveness.

TO CHANGE
ANYTHING THAT
HAPPENED TO
ME WOULD BE
TO CHANGE THE
COURSE OF MY LIFE.

THIRTY-ONE

THERE IS NOTHING TO FORGIVE

IN APRIL of 2018 we were vacationing in Florida for our 15th anniversary. Years have passed since I fell in love with my wife. Years have passed since I began to learn the meaning of love. Years since I inflicted pain on the one being who never hurt me. Years of working on proving myself worthy of her trust again. Years of trying to forgive myself.

She told me many times that she had forgiven me. She was never the same after the dark night of her soul, but her love was apparent. She did not leave me. She did not abandon me emotionally. She patched up her broken heart and allowed me back into it.

At times I was still a bull in the china shop of our lives, often making a mess of things, bringing my insecurities and inadequacies in. Still locking up and withdrawing when she needed me while knowing that she needed my closeness the most. Still emotionally constipated. Improved, but still afflicted by my past.

She was patient with me.

I felt forgiven.

But I still judged myself.

One evening, by the side of the pool at the Ritz Carlton hotel, she leaned over and said something that shook my world like a ten-point earthquake. While I was working on myself, she was going through a rebirth of her own. She too wanted complete freedom from the painful memories of the past.

"I want to be the person I used to be before all this pain," she would tell me. "It seems that forgiveness alone is not cutting it. The pain creeps back up at the most unexpected times. I do not want to live like this for the rest of my life. And I do not want to keep waiting for it to subside on its own."

She kept working on it, digging, meditating, releasing, forgiving, and searching for a way that no one told us existed. A way to turn off the pain from continuously miring her soul. On our anniversary, sitting by the pool, she finally broke out of the cocoon of that pain for good.

"Demetrye," she said quietly so only the two of us could hear. "I love you."

"I love you too," I said, treating it as any other "I love you" I had heard from her over the years.

"And I thank you."

"Thank me for what?"

"Thank you for the pain you've caused."

I did not have to ask what pain she was talking about. It was the pain that changed her and us forever. But what did she mean? Her thanking me for my betrayal sounded irrational. I felt confused and disoriented, so I simply stared at her.

"I thought I needed to forgive you this whole time. And I

THERE IS NOTHING TO FORGIVE

worked hard on doing just that. I worked hard on letting go," she continued. "But the pain still came back. Sometimes at the most unexpected and unwelcomed moments. And it still hurts, as if it happened yesterday. Not as often, but it does. It seems that there is no escaping from it. So I know that forgiveness alone does not set us free. At least not me. Forgiveness releases the offender, but not the offended in many ways. Those who suffered go on hurting, even after they forgive. So I know that there has to be more. I've been searching and looking for a deeper meaning to this pain. A better explanation. I think I finally got it.

"There is nothing to forgive! Nothing! I now understand that, unconsciously, whether of my own accord or jointly with a divine master plan, I orchestrated my whole life to be exactly what it turned out to be. Pain included.

"There are no accidents. I cannot tell you why I chose this path, but I did. But each encounter, each relationship, each pain and discomfort, was orchestrated by me ... for me. Maybe for some greater purpose. Maybe just because. But I am no one's victim."

I stared at her blankly. What crazy Kool-Aid was she drinking? Was it her way to cope with the pain and hurt? Is she trying to justify my offense to justify her staying?

"All I can tell you is this," she continued. "I feel that my life had to happen this way, and it had to involve certain players to turn out just as it did. You were one of them. I feel that you and I had a celestial agreement, way before we were born on this planet, and I asked you to play your role, the role you played so beautifully in my life.

"You probably hated the idea of hurting me, but I must have been convincing because I always get what I want. You agreed. You did your part, as did everyone else in my life. So, instead of blaming you and distancing myself from you by becoming the person your pain created, I want to thank you. Thank you for playing your role and doing your part. You are free. There is nothing for me to forgive because you only did what I asked."

I sat dumbfounded. What just happened? Did I just get the presidential pardon? Everything is forgiven and forgotten? This woman is thanking me for my betrayal! How could it be?

I hated feeling punished and guilty, but it was all I had known. A healthy dose of guilt kept me on the straight and narrow path, as it does for so many of us. Self-loathing and guilt were my life companions, and now Elena was cutting them loose, setting me free, as she had done so many times before. Once again, she was letting me start over with a clean slate. I was willing to accept a clean slate from my daughter—a soul I had not harmed or broken, but from Elena … I did not feel I deserved it. Yet, here she was offering it and inviting me to see myself through her eyes of unconditional love.

If I accept her invitation, what am I to do? If she forgives me unconditionally, where does that leave me with myself? Where does it leave me with all those who hurt me? I think it's safe to say that we are all conditioned by our culture, religion, and our parents to accept the feeling of guilt when we do wrong as a just wage for transgressions. Don't we deserve it after all? In the Bible, you will read, "For the wages of sin is death." In the justice system, the guilty party must pay restitution or serve a sentence to pay penance for their wrongdoings. We are used to accepting a punishment more than forgiveness. And never absolution. How could I go against what has been ingrained in me to accept and then grant unconditional forgiveness?

And could it be that my reluctance to accept Elena's unconditional forgiveness and acceptance was because deep inside I was afraid to let go of shame and guilt because I simply did not know what to do with love without punishment? During all the years I was raised by Tessie and Anne, their love was always commingled with hurt, abuse, shame, and humiliation. It was hard for me to imagine that there was love without pain. So when Elena came into my life I was unconsciously forcing her to fit that pattern. Was I finally at the point where I could accept love for the sake of love? Was I ready to believe that I was worthy of it? Worthy to feel wanted, needed, loved, and cherished just for being me?

Love without conditions.

This would mean that I could extend the same love to myself without further need for punishment.

Much like Elena, I spent my life forgiving. Forgiving my parents, forgiving Tracy, forgiving the teachers who belittled me, forgiving friends who turned on me. Forgiving only to feel the familiar pain they caused wreck my heart over and over when the memories would sneak up at the most unexpected times. If Elena is setting me free, if I forgive myself unconditionally, do I do the same for my abusers?

Whatever Kool-Aid my wife drank to get to this revelation, I wanted it. I too wanted that release toward everyone I blamed for my misfortunes, including myself.

In mere moments, conflicting emotions crushed my mind and my heart. I was confused. I was appalled at the idea. Yet I was elated. It hurt to let go of my guilt and shame. It was a part of my identity, like chains wrapped around my psyche, pulling me down to the bottom of the ocean without a possibility of escape. But as I took in the meaning of Elena's words, after the first crashing wave of disbelief and guilt, I came up for air. My subconscious mind was responding to her pardon faster than my frontal cortex could formulate words. The weight of guilt and stress was lifting. The chains were unlocked. I was free. I could finally breathe. Now, I was jumping, feet first, into the ocean of abolition of my sins and radical love.

This was the key to my freedom! Everything else that led up to this moment was only a prelude, a beautiful setup, a slowly building crescendo of my life. And this ... this was the resolution! The final chord of the symphony of healing, and the first note of the masterpiece to my happily ever after.

There were still questions, a lot of them, if I were to accept her pardon.

There is nothing to forgive. But how do I let go of the past? How do I go beyond forgiveness? How do I heal the pain of my past? I had a laundry list of questions.

Many conversations with Elena followed. I wanted her to break down for me what she did for herself. She did it in a way only a scientist could. (I did not mention this before, but Elena is a science geek. She consumes math, physics, quantum physics, neuroscience and many other exact sciences as others would consume romance novels.) So, she broke it down for me.

If I were to accept the fact that I orchestrated my own life, including the pain I endured and the pain I caused, there were steps that I could take to release the brokenness I accrued over the years of my human existence.

In the quantum field, filled with countless possibilities, there is no time. There is only the present moment. Anything is possible. No past or future. Everything always is. Past, present, and future are always in the now. This means I could access any reality I wanted in the now.

It is a time travel of sorts. Not the kind that involves a time machine that could transport your body along a time-space continuum. A time travel of a different kind. I could

THERE IS NOTHING TO FORGIVE

reach into my past as easily as I could choose one of the future possibilities.

If there is no past or future and I always have access to my emotions from the past, which evidently I did frequently when it came to my memories since I still could feel the pain of betrayal and childhood abandonment as if they happened yesterday, then it would stand to reason that I could time travel emotionally. I could reach the younger version of myself and help him break free from the hurts that accumulated in his soul by letting him know two things: (1) that his pain is a part of a grander plan, and (2) that everything will work out beautifully for him in the end.

At first it was hard to wrap my mind around this quantum-physics-neuroscience hack talk, but I was game to give it a go. So one night, I took my meditation mask and went to time travel, to get my freedom.

I went to each moment of my life when I was abused, when I was left behind, when I was neglected, and I visited with the younger versions of me in those moments. One moment to the next, one pain to another. Until I finally landed at the place where the young me spent a lot of his time.

There he is, little Dee, barely three, sitting at the top of the stairs, screaming after his mom. She did not look back as the door slammed shut behind her. He is crying, screaming, begging. The apartment reeks of Raid. Little Kat is already lost in play with the roommate kids. Little Dee is all alone, crying inconsolably.

Suddenly he feels a presence around him. He does not know what to call it. Years later, as he grows up in a religious environment, he will call it God or maybe angels. But he knows he is not alone.

As I visit with him, I realize it was neither God nor angels that he felt. It is the thirty-nine-year-old version of myself visiting with him, watching him, being an observer.

It is finally time to step out of the shadows.

"Hi, Dee," I say softly.

"Hi," he responds, spreading snot across his oval face with his left arm, still sniffling.

"How are you feeling?" I venture to ask.

"Sad," he responds.

"Why so sad?"

"My mommy just left me. And I don't like this place."

"Are you scared, Dee?"

"Yes."

"What do you feel now?" I reach for him, drawing him in.

"I feel okay. I am not afraid of you."

"Do you know who I am, Dee?"

"No." He is looking up at me quizzically with his brown almond-shaped eyes.

"I am you, over thirty years from now."

"You are?" he asks curiously.

"Yes." I smile, cupping his little face in my hands. "Do I look a little like you?"

"Yes," he responds, relaxing into my arms.

"Well, that's because this is how you'll look when you're older."

"Really?" His face lights up with hope. He seems impressed.

"And guess what, Dee?" I continue.

"What?" He is excited.

"This," I respond, pointing at his surroundings, "this won't last forever. I promise you. Things will get much better for you."

"Really?"

I can see peace and comfort wash over his toddler-size body. Suddenly, he has hope that his pain and suffering will end. He smiles at me. The thirty-nine-year-old me feels a release of emotions. My chest opens up. I can breathe.

I grab his little hand and lead him down the stairs where he saw his mother disappear into the streets so many times. I push the door open and, to our surprise, the dangerous streets of my childhood are not there to greet us.

Instead, the door flings open to a field pregnant with ripe grain. Above us, a bright blue sky. Both of us, Little Dee and Big Dee are surprised by the scenery. We stand speechless for a moment. Then we jump into the field, giggling, laughing, feeling free. We do cartwheels, clown around, and play.

I grab him and hoist him onto my shoulders. We start running. He is squealing with delight. He is finally experiencing the childhood he was never afforded to have. We are lost in play for what seems like hours.

I finally put him down and take a few steps back to watch him and absorb the scenery. Little Dee is beaming. There is no more sadness or fear on his face. His eyes dance with trust and mischief—the same kind that I see in my daughter's eyes daily.

He runs toward me fast and I stretch my arms out to catch him. Instead, he vanishes into me. Completely. We are now one and the same. The boy in me is happy. The boy in me is safe. The boy in me is whole.

Tears pouring down my face. I, the thirty-nine-year-old Dee, am now filled with love and wholeness. I just had my perfect childhood moment.

It was in that moment that I finally accepted all the good, the bad, and the ugly that made me who I am. To change anything that happened to me, which I used to wish for often, would be to change the course of my life. To change one thing would be to rob me of my present joy, rob me of my life, my identity, my wife, and my daughter. I could not fathom being anywhere other than where I am, anyone other than who I am. The life I now have is a beautiful one. Whether I felt like a victim or a villain, each step brought me to this place.

At that moment, I accepted everything life had given me. It happened for me, not to me. I accepted each gift, peaceful and violent alike, thanking life for its generosity.

There was nothing to change. No one to blame. No one to forgive. Everything happened, as if by design, to bring me into the perfect place in my present life.

A friend of mine once said, "The highest form of forgiveness is the authentic recognition that everything served you and there is nothing to forgive."

I finally got it! On a deep heart and gut level. I got it! There was nothing and no one to forget or forgive. Tessie, Edward, Anne, Liza, John, Tracy, and everyone who ever inflicted pain on me were only players in the story of my life, just like I was in Elena's. They were to be thanked, not forgiven. I could finally release them from the prison of my heart where they had been shackled and judged by me for decades. I was free! They can now be free too.

Tessie was not the enemy. She was an ally. I allowed my pain and my memories of her to cripple me and my relationships. Now I could see that when she dropped me and Kat at strangers' homes, she was not neglecting us. Rather, she was protecting us. Protecting us from herself and her demons. It was her way of keeping us safe.

Now, in my memories, Little Dee does not have to cry after a mom-turned-whore anymore. He is beaming from ear to ear knowing she is keeping evil away from him. His heart is filled with gratitude.

When I came back from my time travel to the present,

THERE IS NOTHING TO FORGIVE

I realized, much like Elena, that my life was designed by a great force. Each moment in my life was picked by this grand master for me to become who I am, to be where I am. Perhaps that force, that master was me.

I was finally free to let go of my prison and let everyone I held in it free. I would start with my mother. She needed to know. So I wrote her a letter.

Mom,

It's been twenty-nine years since I last saw you. Twenty-nine years since we last spoke. The time has gone by so fast and so much has happened.

The last time I saw you was at Aunt Liza and Uncle John's house before you went to Yemassee. At the time, I asked myself: "Why does she have to go?" Now I know.

I remember calling you Mom, even though it displeased Aunt Liza. I remember hugging you and telling you that I love you, not knowing it would be the last time.

There is so much that transpired in the little time we had together. So much pain and turmoil. I blamed you often for abandoning me. Leaving me behind. Not wanting me. But things have changed since then. So, I want to take a little bit of time to show you how your leaving me was the greatest gift you could have ever given.

Since you left, I discovered that our life is not black and white, making one good and the other bad; rather, the black and white are the duality of who we are, the yin and yang of life. One cannot exist without the other. You can't have the good without the bad, joy without sorrow, thrill of victory without the agony of defeat. Our life is lived in contrast between the two, and that is what makes it worth living.

My last memory of you was me watching you sleep on the couch at the Browns' home. You groaned a few times, as if you were having a nightmare. When I recalled this moment a few weeks back, I became angry. Angry that you didn't provide Kat and me with the life we should have had—a life of safety and love, life filled with provision and shelter by you, not from you. I felt alone when you left. As I reflected on my own emotions over the last few weeks, I opened my heart to seeing a different side to this story—your side.

You did not know how to give us safety or love, how to shelter us from the world or from yourself, so you gave us the thing that was the closest to it—you placed us with a family that would care for us. You placed us with a family that would send us to a private school so we could receive the best education their money could afford. Although you did not know how to express love, you gave it the best way you knew how by finding us a family who would never leave me alone the way you did. They would be there with me through thick and thin, and through the hell I put them through as a teenager. Because of you leaving, I was never alone.

Each time I was physically abused, I felt that you abandoned me time and time again. And each time it hurt so badly that I could barely breathe. Each time I remembered you leaving me with strangers, as I screamed for you to come back, it hurt. It hurt when I remembered that you wouldn't so much as glance back at me. But for whatever reason, I now see that you didn't abandon me the time you said goodbye for the last time. You left me in better hands than yours. While not without pain, I haven't felt abandonment since.

When I saw you last, sleeping so restlessly, I had a hunch that it would be the last time. For reasons unknown, when I looked at you, I felt okay. I was at peace.

I never had peace with you, Mom. I was never at ease. I was always scared of where you might drag us next, wondering who we would spend the night with. Would you stay with us or disappear again, like a woman possessed in search of something precious she might have lost? Fear all around. Constant. Ever present.

As I walked away from your sleeping body that day, I didn't feel the same fear and uncertainty anymore. I felt safe and at peace.

THERE IS NOTHING TO FORGIVE

Life is filled with dualities. Love and pain, fear and peace, joy and sorrow. If it weren't for your choices, I wouldn't be where I am today—married to the most wonderful woman in the world and a father to the most beautiful daughter a man could ask for. Unplanned and unbeknownst to you—you had a part to play in all of this. If you stayed with us, as was my wish, I wouldn't have the life I now proudly and joyfully possess. If you stayed and fought to get us back, our lives would have been worse off. God knows, I might have even ended up behind bars, like my father and brother.

I can now see and appreciate that you did what you knew best. You told Kat before leaving us for the last time that you did not know what love was. However, I now see that you found a way to love us by leaving. So ... thank you!

Thanks to you, pain and joy were inseparable twins to get me to where I am now. Thank you. Thank you for being brave in sharing your pain with me, so I can now live a life of my dreams.

I miss you greatly. I wish you could see me now. I have a hunch that you probably can. I love you.
Dee

MY PAST IS
NOTHING BUT
A STEP ON A
JOURNEY OF A
THOUSAND MILES.

THIRTY-TWO

BUT THERE IS ROOM FOR FORGIVENESS

IF YOU are like me, a million objections might be flying through your frontal cortex after reading the previous chapter.

"Great story, Demetrye! But I call bulls**t!" your mind is hollering. You might even feel tempted to set this book on fire or leave a really bad review that would read, "This is some New Age bulls**t!" I get it!

Is there really nothing to forgive?

This revelation freed Elena and it freed me from years of pain, shame, and suffering. It allowed me to have gratitude for each moment of my life, good or bad. It certainly was like music to the villain part of me that had hurt others.

Is there really nothing to forgive? Because, if there isn't, doesn't this give license to the offenders to keep inflicting pain on others? Does accepting life as if we designed it mean that we accept and pardon violence committed against us and others, regardless of how horrific it was? Does Elena's releasing me give me the permission to do more of what I had done to her? If I did it, wouldn't that also be a part of her unconscious life-plan and was meant to be? If everything that happens does so by some grand design, does it give me the permission to commit a murder or rob a bank?

If we accept our lives as is, is there still a need for forgiveness or repentance? And ultimately, if there is nothing to forgive, are we still right to desire an apology from those who hurt and offended us?

These were the questions I had to wrestle with and work out for myself. I am certain that these are the same objections swirling through your head right now (especially if you are of religious convictions, because you are taught to forgive no matter the cost, even if you struggle with pain after forgiving).

I am sure that we all can make a list a mile long why we should not forgive and forget. Or forgive in word, but keep suffering internally. In our minds, it would be a way for us to keep punishing those who hurt us, even if they are oblivious to the very fact that we are still thinking about them or the pain they inflicted.

But, as the saying goes, holding onto unforgiveness is like drinking poison hoping someone else will die.

Forgiveness is defined as a conscious, deliberate decision to release feelings of resentment and vengeance toward those who harm us, regardless of whether they deserve our forgiveness or not.

Raised in religion, I learned that, in religious circles, forgiveness means wiping the slate clean, pardoning the offender, or cancelling their emotional debt. Even by these definitions, forgiveness does not mean that the offender will change. But that's one thing that we all want—for them to change, even if that means that our forgiveness must be the catalyst for that to happen, and then to repent and ask us for forgiveness. (It's okay. You can admit to this, because no one can hear your thoughts. Dare to be honest with yourself.)

We are taught to forgive. In fact, we are commanded to. You cannot go to church without hearing something like this straight out of Matthew: "... and forgive us our sins, as we have forgiven those who sin against us."

Or: "Then Peter came to him and asked, 'How often should I forgive someone who sins against me? Seven times?'

"'No, not seven times,' Jesus replied, 'but seventy times seven!'"

Religious or not, do we really need to forgive? Do we really have to forgive?

Let's say we decide that we must forgive no matter what. Do we forgive for ourselves or for the offenders? When we forgive, do we forgive to make them or ourselves feel better? Do we forgive so they could repent and become better people? Do we forgive to release them and ourselves from the pain they inflicted, or to get a checkmark that we have done it because we were "good and loyal servants" of our convictions?

Most importantly, if we forgive others, do we remember to extend the same grace of forgiving and absolving ourselves for being victims and villains alike?

Over seventy percent of the women Elena works with have suffered some form of trauma—emotional, psychological, physical, and even sexual. These women, while trying to make do with the remnants of their lives, struggle with forgiveness. More often than not, they struggle with forgiving themselves. They feel that their pain is somehow their fault. That they deserved it. Although mentally they can reason it away, they feel that somehow they allowed the bad to happen to them and, therefore they are to be blamed. So, while forgiving their offenders, they find it harder to forgive and love themselves.

I felt that way too.

I had lived through the metamorphosis from victim to villain. I was hurt, so I hurt others. I was punished, so I punished the person who loved me the most. If I were forgiven, I would have to forgive myself, which I found to be the hardest of the two. So I understand if you struggle with the idea that "there is nothing to forgive." I am still a student of this philosophy, so, I get it!

In the meantime, as I accept my life with all of its gifts daily, I find that there is still a place for forgiveness when it comes to immediate offenses and poor decisions I or others make. If I raise my voice when I shouldn't, "I'm sorry. Please forgive me." If someone cuts me off in traffic, "I forgive you." If my daughter misbehaves, I teach her the art of apology. And even if someone hurts me deeply, I extend forgiveness to them for their and my sake. I do this until I can say: "I've learned from this. This made me stronger. This too is a part of the invisible plan for my life. I can let go of the pain and live in gratitude for this moment." This allows me to bridge the gap between the two philosophies and have a joy-filled life.

Collectively, we are not raised to believe that we are responsible for creating the very world around us, like many have believed for centuries before us. We are not raised to believe that everything that happens, happens for us not to us. And even if we did, millions of those around us still do not, so we get influenced by their beliefs.

Perhaps there is still room for forgiveness, but forgiving

in a way that would give us our power back. Combining situational forgiveness for our daily screwups, as in "I'm sorry I was a jerk to you and disrespected you," with "there is nothing to forgive" for bigger situations in life that we do not have apparent control over, makes for a powerful combination.

If anything, the "there is nothing to forgive" philosophy gives us our power back. It puts us back in the driver's seat of our lives. It makes us creators, opens our eyes wide to observe the world we construct. It lets us be responsible and live on purpose, rather than living with a sense of helplessness, victims of a force bigger than ourselves. This way, we become more diligent about making decisions with long-term implications in mind. Instead of flailing day-to-day, when we realize we chose our lives on purpose, we can begin to make our decisions on purpose too. Choose our careers on purpose. Choose our partners on purpose. Choose our friends and the places we live on purpose.

Perhaps subscribing to the idea that there is nothing to forgive could release us from feeling forced to forgive our offenders. We can let go of our hurt and release ourselves from the hold of their offense and leave them to deal with their own demons. Their own need for the abolishing of their wrongdoings. And for justice to be served. This does not prevent us from forgiving and accepting ourselves, freeing ourselves to live in power and purpose.

To live with an attitude of "there is nothing to forgive" does not mean we refuse to go through the full spectrum of human emotions. We do not have to numb ourselves to cope with the pain and pretend that we are happy to be hurt. We still feel the emotions of pain, anger, disappointment, and we still grieve. We let our human emotions run their course and serve their purpose. However, we do not stay in these emotions forever. Doing so would be damaging to our spiritual, emotional, and physical health. So we need to feel whatever helps us get through acute pain and trauma, releasing the emotions from our bodies so they do not get stuck and make us sick and bitter.

However, once this acute phase is over, we can choose to move into gratitude and look for lessons even in the worst situations. Doing otherwise would only leave us stuck in pain and victimhood. Doing otherwise would also teach our children victimhood, limiting their ability to be in charge of their lives. Doing otherwise would create generations of broken, helpless people. And, as humanity, we've already had our fill of that.

If you feel brave and want to subscribe to the philosophy of "there is nothing to forgive" and start taking full ownership of what is happening in your life, the transition will not happen overnight. It will not be easy. The old conditioning in you might want to fight you. You might still get stuck in the guilt-shame-blame, I-must-forgive-or-expect-an-apology cycle. I know I still do. And that's okay.

Life is not about achieving perfection. It's about our continual effort to move in the right direction—the direction of joy, love, peace, oneness, and purpose. The direction of being responsible for our choices and our lives. At least it is for me. And when living out my newly adopted philosophy gets especially hard, I practice hoʻoponopono to release myself from guilt and shame and to put myself back into the creator mode of my life.

Hoʻoponopono is an ancient Hawaiian practice of cleansing, healing, and righting ourselves with ourselves and those around us. Indigenous Hawaiians understood that to harbor resentment against others or oneself hurts the person who refuses to forgive, essentially causing sickness, whether of the body, mind, or the community. They also believed that the world we live in is that of our internal making, so, essentially, we are responsible for all our experiences. It allows us to have full creative abilities over our lives and the responsibilities that come with them.

The Hawaiian word ho'oponopono comes from ho'o, *to make*, and pono, *right*. The repetition of the word pono means *"doubly right"* or being right with both self and others. Simply put, ho'oponopono is a process by which we can forgive others to whom we are connected and ourselves in order to heal.

Ho'oponopono can be practiced face to face with the people who hurt us or whom we hurt, or it can be a process we experience individually, within ourselves only.

Ho'oponopono is practiced in four simple steps: repentance, forgiveness, gratitude, and love. The process is put into a simple prayer, which I often say to myself: *I'm sorry. Please forgive me. Thank you. I love you.*

I'm sorry: It's a way to say we realize we are responsible for the issue or pain in our life, whether by physical deed or in our mind, and we are remorseful for causing it.

Please forgive me: We get to ask ourselves, or others, to be forgiven and released.

Thank you: We thank ourselves, or others, for what happened, the pain caused and endured, and for forgiving us and letting go.

I love you: We get to show love to whoever or whatever is serving us—our offenders, situations, our past, or ourselves. We get to release the love from our hearts, because there is nothing as powerful as love. In fact, forgiveness is not possible without love. That's why most attempts at forgiveness fail. Because we find it nearly impossible to truly embrace the offender with love and the offense they caused.

When the regrets over my misdeeds set in or the pain caused by others washes over me, I hoʻoponopono myself:

I'm sorry, Demetrye, for all the things I have caused to make you and the ones you love suffer. Please forgive me, as I now acknowledge my role in the pain. I take ownership of it. Thank you for being here for me through thick and thin and not giving up on life, on hope and love. Things will get better as I do better. I love you for staying alive and for trying again. I love you for creating my life on purpose.

There is no way for us to remember all the hurts of the past in one moment, even when we are ready to move forward with an attitude of "there is nothing to forgive." However, when we are ready, our heart and our mind will bring memories of the events that need to be released, accepted, and assimilated in a state of gratitude. Memories that had been locked away in the deepest recesses of our being will arise. Not one to waste. Each with a gift inside it.

As it happens for me and memories float into my conscious mind, I spend time letting go of my sins and the sins of others. Some of the memories invite me to work through my emotions before healing each and adding them to my gratitude list. I get a chance to examine them, to ask myself questions, to "walk the walk."

For example, at times I find that a part of me still craves an apology from those who had done me wrong. There are times I still want Anne, my ultimate mother figure, to acknowledge the abuse she inflicted on me. As the memories of my childhood float to the top for me to work through, the part of me that was raised to be a victim, the part that is not yet ready to transcend still wants closure. And when that happens, I work through the process to bring healing and

BUT THERE IS ROOM FOR FORGIVENESS

closure.

I called Anne once, when I was working through one such memory, and asked her a simple question. "Why were you so harsh with me and Kat when we were little?"

"If you are looking for an apology, Dee," she responded, "you won't get it. I had to do what I did to make you into the man you are today."

The old me would be hurt, angry, and disappointed. However, the new me, the one that has taken his power back, the one that grew from a victim to villain to victor, knew that I must move on and transcend. That I was to take my creative power back. That I was to thank my life and every player in it for doing their part, including Anne. Directly or indirectly, on purpose or by chance, all things that happened to me ultimately made me into the man who is penning these words right now. For that, I am grateful.

As memories came to me for healing, I forgave and released Tessie, Anne, Liza, John, Edward, and Tracy. I released them from the prison of my mind. And I released myself from the prison of the pain they put me in and the pain I inflicted on others.

I am now a practicing believer of "there is nothing to forgive" philosophy.

When and if the pain of the past comes, each time fainter than the time before, I go through the process of releasing it, accepting my past as if it was designed by me and for me. I hoʻoponopono myself and others and move on.

Moving on is not hard because I find that forgiveness and acceptance do not mean condoning, excusing, or forgetting the offenders. They have their own demons to fight and their own lessons to learn. My forgiveness does not absolve them from their need to get right with themselves, others, or the divine in them.

As I struggled to accept Elena's forgiveness at first, I realized that she did not absolve me from feeling the pain my actions caused or to do her more harm. Rather, she released herself from the aftermath of my choices. She took her power back. My choices no longer define her. Her emotions are free of my deeds. Whether she stays or leaves, loves or hates, it would be because she made the choice. Understanding this gave me the power to forgive others and myself.

It's a daily practice. I forgive those who hurt me and release them. I thank them for the role they played in my life.

It's a daily practice. I forgive myself for the wrongs I have done, never to be repeated. I thank myself for the lessons I learned.

It's a daily practice. I thank everyone who has forgiven me for teaching me love.

It's a daily practice. A practice to keep the freedom that I achieved.

As I practice my freedom daily, I've emerged from my guilt and pain. Metamorphosed from victim to villain to victor to freedom. Now I am free to live my life without pain holding me back. Free from living in guilt and unforgiveness toward others and myself. Free to choose from the unlimited number of possibilities the quantum field has to offer. Free from guilt and unforgiveness, I know what I will choose every single time—accepting myself and my life as it is. My past is nothing but a step on a journey of a thousand miles.

As I live out my "there is nothing to forgive" journey, I realize that we all can and should do better. I found that once I learned that I was responsible for my own life, that I was the master of my own fate, and that I am the only one who determines whether I live in pleasure or misery, I became even more responsible for planning and living my every moment on purpose. I take full responsibility for my deeds, my beliefs, and what I get from my life.

Whether we accept our lives in all their brokenness with a "there is nothing to forgive" attitude, or if we are staunch believers in forgiveness, either way we must go beyond the surface of these philosophies. We must become faithful practitioners of our convictions. We must dig deep and excavate every dark part of us and our past to examine, to accept or release.

We can choose to forgive, but first, we must accept ourselves as we are, without further shame or judgement, so that we can become whole. Whole to live our lives, to fulfill our purpose. As we each make our healing our focus, we won't have to point out the faults and offenses of others. We will allow them to come to their own revelation of what repentance and forgiveness means to them, as we do so for ourselves.

This is how we can heal generational wounds and become the springboard for future generations to create a more whole human experience that abounds with forgiveness, love, peace, and abundance. This is how forgiveness can reverberate back in time, throughout past generations, to heal our collective and individual wounds. I believe that if and when we release this forgiveness, there's going to be a collective exhale from pain. With pain gone, there is no more generational "curse." There is no more hatred, victimhood, or division. Not in ourselves, our families, our communities, or our countries.

Each individual can start the work in themselves. Each family. Each ethnic group. This way we will heal ourselves and the world around us. When we shed victimhood, we will be able to claim our power and create our own future—personal and collective. As we do, we will reclaim not only our power, but also our dignity and unity.

If we can see that our future and the future of humanity hinges on our ability to accept each experience—painful and joyful alike—with gratitude, we would not need reparations or special provisions to get ahead in life. We would not need pity or handouts, because we would remember just how powerful we are. We could then achieve our greatness based on our identity and our merits.

Only by having learned from the past and becoming grateful for it can we create our collective and personal future based on forgiveness and power, rather than the pain of our ancestral and individual past. From this power, we can usher the next evolution of humanity.

However, as I walk out my freedom daily, this is what I have come to realize:

The kind of freedom and power I describe in this book is not for everyone. It is only for those brave enough to practice forgiveness and acceptance of self and others, those who are ready to forge ahead in the face of our fickle emotions. It is for those who are willing to do the work, those unwilling to stay in their victimhood, those ready to become creators of their own destiny and emotions.

For those who are willing, we learn that freedom is achieved from within, not without. There is nothing to forgive, but so much to accept and be grateful for. And, if there is nothing to forgive, we can be students of both pleasure and pain. Equally grateful for both. If there is nothing to forgive, there is nothing to hold us back.

EVERYTHING
I NEED IS
ALWAYS
WITHIN ME.

THIRTY-THREE

THE GIFT OF LOVE

I WAS thirty-nine when my life came full circle. I shed skins. Instead of spending years in therapy or popping pills to cope with past trauma, instead of giving up on life or ending up in prison like Edward and his son, I became the man I used to dream about—free, strong, gentle, understanding, loyal. I am a man who finally knows how to love and to be loved. If I can do it, so can anyone else.

I am not perfect. I am still human, filled with shortcomings. I celebrate them as much as I celebrate my accomplishments. Perfection is not what I strive for these days. Happiness is. Fulfillment is. Peace is. Love is.

In the months following my first quantum trip, I took many more trips into my past, collapsing the time, healing my inner child, filling the Tessie-size void in my heart with love and security. Each time I came back from my quantum time travel, I became more of the person I wanted to be.

SON OF A WHORE

I let go of my hurt and embraced my past to create the man I am today. Everything I need is always within me: love, gratitude, generosity, creativity. My past, present, and my future—all are always within me. Each moment is pregnant with a new gift, should I be brave enough to reach for it and unwrap it. I am now empowered to make a choice to either allow the perception of my past to dictate how to live my life or to become the cause of everything that happens in it and be the creator of my future. I now always choose the latter.

And now, in some of my time travels, I have conversations with Tessie. During one of them we had the mother-son dance we never got to experience. As I held her tiny body, her hand resting in mine, she spoke to me.

"Our story needs to be told, Dee," she said. "Now that you know the truth, share this truth. The good, the bad, and the very ugly. There is nothing to hide. Save someone else from the pain we both endured. Set them free, like you've been set free. Help them find their freedom."

"Mom," I told her, "if I do this, I will have to tell the whole truth. I can't hold anything back."

"You have my blessing, Dee. Tell it all."

As she vanished into the vault of my mind, I could still feel her presence and finally feel the mother's love I had craved most of my life radiating in me. The woman who could not give or receive love while living found a way to gift it to me from beyond the grave.

"Tell it all!"

Her name is Tessie. She is my mother. And this is our story.

FOR A VISUAL JOURNEY OF
SON OF A WHORE, VISIT
WWW.DEMETRYEISOLDI.COM.

ABOUT THE AUTHORS

Demetrye Isoldi is a survivor of heart-wrenching childhood trauma and abuse. His mother tried to abort him with a wire hanger. His father tried to suffocate him when he was only one year old. His home life was steeped in neglect, violence, and abuse. Eventually, his mother abandoned her tumultuous relationship to pursue her own happiness, and left Demetrye with strangers to a life of pain and struggle. However, Demetrye refused to be a victim. Instead of following his parents' path of abuse, violence, and destitution, Demetrye chose to use his brokenness as fuel for the rest of his life by forging his own path to success, freedom, happiness, and love.

In contrast, Elena Isoldi Medici was raised by loving parents and grew up in a nurturing environment. Despite experiencing religious persecution in the USSR, she knew no limits because she had the love and support of her family. The first time Elena experienced brokenness was when her world collided with Demetrye's. Rather than running from the pain, she embraced it and used it as a creative force to construct a life filled with hope, forgiveness, and purpose.

Refusing victimhood, both Elena and Demetrye have used their pain to fuel their passion and strengthen their relationship. Together, they have built a successful life and health coaching practice that has touched thousands of lives around the world. *Son of a Whore* is their homage to the resilience of the human spirit and fortitude in the face of extreme hardships and trauma.

Demetrye and Elena delight in raising their wonderful daughter, Isabella, along with their rambunctious cavapoo, Milo.

Learn more and start your personal transformation journey at www.demetryeisoldi.com.

www.ingramcontent.com/pod-product-compliance
Lightning Source LLC
Chambersburg PA
CBHW071223080526
44587CB00013BA/1478